TAIWAN 101

TAIWAN 101

Studying, Working, and Traveling in Today's Taiwan

MATTHEW B. CHRISTENSEN
HENRIETTA YANG, PHD

ROWMAN & LITTLEFIELD
Lanham • Boulder • New York • London

Published by Rowman & Littlefield
An imprint of The Rowman & Littlefield Publishing Group, Inc.
4501 Forbes Boulevard, Suite 200, Lanham, Maryland 20706
www.rowman.com

86-90 Paul Street, London EC2A 4NE

Copyright © 2024 by The Rowman & Littlefield Publishing Group, Inc.

All rights reserved. No part of this book may be reproduced in any form or by any electronic or mechanical means, including information storage and retrieval systems, without written permission from the publisher, except by a reviewer who may quote passages in a review.

British Library Cataloguing in Publication Information Available

Library of Congress Cataloging-in-Publication Data

Names: Christensen, Matthew B., author. | Yang, Henrietta, author.
Title: Taiwan 101 : studying, working, and traveling in today's Taiwan / Matthew Christensen and Henrietta Yang, PhD.
Description: Lanham : Rowman & Littlefield, [2024] | Includes bibliographical references and index. | Summary: "This book provides a practical, up-to-date, guide to navigating life in Taiwan. It is not a travel guidebook, but rather provides detailed information for the foreign resident in Taiwan. It provides information from renting apartments, taking care of your daily needs, what and where to eat, Taiwanese business culture, and how to get around"—Provided by publisher.
Identifiers: LCCN 2023038427 (print) | LCCN 2023038428 (ebook) | ISBN 9781538187807 (cloth) | ISBN 9781538187814 (epub)
Subjects: LCSH: Noncitizens—Taiwan—Life skills guides. | Taiwan—Social life and customs—1975– | Taiwan—Guidebooks.
Classification: LCC DS798.965 .C575 2024 (print) | LCC DS798.965 (ebook) | DDC 305.9/06910951249--dc23/eng/20230908
LC record available at https://lccn.loc.gov/2023038427
LC ebook record available at https://lccn.loc.gov/2023038428

CONTENTS

1	Why Taiwan?	1
2	Who Lives in Taiwan?	17
3	Getting Around in Taiwan	35
4	Taiwan's Food Scene	55
5	Living in Taiwan	85
6	Studying in Taiwan	105
7	Working and Interning in Taiwan	125
8	Taiwan's Diverse Geography	135
	Notes	151
	Index	155
	About the Authors	163

1

WHY TAIWAN?

The first time I (Matt) visited Taiwan, around 2012, I had been traveling to Mainland China for a couple decades and was well acclimated to how things are there. Within minutes of arrival in Taipei, I knew I was in a very different place. After dropping off my bags at a delightful little boutique hotel, I was crossing the street heading to the subway station when a large public bus came around the corner. I was ready to sprint to the other side, when the bus came to a slow stop and the driver motioned me to cross. I was astonished, frozen in place. I quickly recovered and scampered across the road, trying to process what just happened. In Mainland China, dealing with traffic can be a much scarier adventure. I found Taiwan to be clean, orderly, modern, convenient, and the people very polite. It reminded me more of Hong Kong, where I had lived previously, than my experiences in Mainland China.

WHAT IS UNIQUE ABOUT TAIWAN?

Taiwan is a vibrant, liberal society with a free press, gender equality, respect for human rights, an excellent education system, convenient and efficient public transportation, a thriving democracy, scenic beauty, friendly people, and a safe environment. It does get quite hot and humid in the summer months, much like Hong Kong and Guangzhou, or Miami and Houston in the United States, but it is an ideal location to study, work, and live.

If you have been to China, you will notice that both Mainland China and Taiwan share many similarities, such as a common ethnic majority (Chinese), similar national languages (Mandarin Chinese), and similar traditional Chinese core values, ethics, and beliefs. However, Taiwan and

A bird's-eye view of Taipei City. *Image courtesy of Henrietta Yang*

Mainland China are different places, ruled by completely different governments. While the government of the People's Republic of China considers Taiwan a renegade province, still part of Mainland China, the Taiwanese consider themselves as a separate, though not quite independent, political entity. Taiwanese, who travel internationally with a different passport from citizens of Mainland China, are governed by democratically elected leaders and are not controlled by the Communist Party in China. Besides politics, probably the primary reason Taiwan feels so different from the Mainland is because of decades of exposure to and influence from outside, mostly the West and Japan. Taiwan is a thoroughly modern, free society with highly educated citizens and an openness that is sometimes lacking in China.

For a Westerner, Taiwan is an easy place to live in Asia. The contrasts with North America and Europe are not as stark, and the modern conveniences available in most North American cities are present throughout Taiwan. Not only is Taiwan physically closer to the West, but the people also have a better understanding of what is going on in the world, and this is reflected in their attitudes and behavior. This awareness is due to an open and free press where information within and outside Taiwan is easily accessible. Though most Taiwanese are thoroughly Chinese, they understand and communicate well with foreigners.

DEEP CHINESE CULTURE

It is often said that, of all Chinese-speaking areas, Taiwan is the most conservative with regard to traditional Chinese Confucian values. In fact,

Taiwan seems to uphold conservative traditional Chinese values more than other Chinese-speaking countries, and it is reflected in the people's attitudes and behaviors. For example, the concept of filial piety, and respect for elders and educators such as teachers and professors, is fundamental to Taiwanese culture. In the Mainland, when the Communists came to power in 1949, especially during the Cultural Revolution era, they attempted to rid people of old, outdated, and traditional values. The party and loyalty to it and its leaders became more important than anything else. China's one-child policy also ran counter to the Confucian value and importance of family. Traditionally, the Chinese had large families; children were considered a blessing. In Taiwan there has never been these kinds of restrictions, and consequently Taiwanese families are typically larger than those on the Mainland, though in recent years the birth rate in Taiwan has dropped significantly due to late marriage, cost of raising a child, and more women joining the workforce.

There has been a long tradition in Chinese culture of religious practice, often in the form of ancestor worship or worshipping folk deities. Because religious practices have never been suppressed in Taiwan, this is still a vibrant part of Taiwanese culture. Other values, like treating others, including strangers, with respect, kindness, and dignity, are quite prevalent in Taiwanese society.

FOREIGN INFLUENCE ON TAIWAN

For most of Taiwan's history, there has been a foreign presence and influence. This goes back centuries to contact with the Dutch, Portuguese, English, Korean, and Japanese. Because of this, Taiwanese culture is unique in that it has embraced various aspects of these foreign cultures, from architecture and food to the willingness of Taiwanese to accept different points of view. Taiwan is unique in its ability to adopt foreign influences and yet remain deeply Chinese in their character. For example, in many of Taipei's neighborhoods, it is easy to see the Japanese-influenced architecture. And even though Japan ruled Taiwan for decades as a colony, Taiwanese are quick to embrace Japanese food, fashions, and a love of Japanese culture. Even today there is a strong Japanese cultural presence in Taiwan, from Japanese teahouses and department stores to the latest electronics and pop culture (i.e., the wildly popular Hello Kitty and Miyazaki's characters such as Totoro).

A Japanese food vendor on a university campus. *Image courtesy of Henrietta Yang*

Taiwanese people tend to be open-minded and well-traveled. Literacy rates are almost 99 percent, and most urban people are well informed about what is going on in the world.[1] As a result, Taiwanese are very open toward foreigners. Taiwanese tend to speak English well, and it is not too difficult to get around with basic English, especially in urban areas.

Because of Taiwan's long-term exposure to the West, there has been a long tradition of Chinese language teaching and study in Taiwan. Before relations with Mainland China were established in 1979, nearly every Westerner that wanted to study Chinese did so in Taiwan. Taiwan universities have been teaching Chinese as a foreign language for a long time. Chinese language programs in Taiwan tend to have more up-to-date pedagogical practices and a more Western-friendly educational culture. For students this means that there are excellent Chinese language programs in Taiwan that have extensive experience teaching foreigners. In addition to well-organized and sound language programs, they are well equipped to deal with all aspects of a study experience, including housing, travel, cultural outings, and so on. Though I (Matt) personally never studied Chinese in Taiwan, I have many students who have, and without exception, they have been very happy with their experiences. Because of the increased challenges of studying in Mainland China, many North American university study programs in China are moving to Taiwan. Taiwan universities are accommodating and can leverage their experience to continue to provide top-quality study programs.

TAIWAN'S RELIGIOUS ATMOSPHERE

Taiwan has an open religious environment with countless Buddhist, Taoist, and Confucian temples, and numerous folk deity temples thrive and are excellent places to learn about traditional Chinese religions without worrying about government censorship or screening. Residents and visitors alike can worship how and when they please. There is also a vibrant Christian population and numerous Christian places of worship, with most Christian denominations represented.

Like Westerners who pray at home or in churches, Taiwanese go to temples to pray or worship at home whenever they need spiritual support or strength. Temples are abundant, some large and bustling and others small and tucked away in residential neighborhoods. In Taiwan there are no entrance fees to enter temples, and temples and religious sites cater to worshippers and not tourists. Ritual worship has been an important part of Taiwanese culture for centuries. It is common to see families with children, young couples, older residents, and just about every other demographic of society worshipping at Taiwan's various temples.

A local temple. *Image courtesy of Matthew B. Christensen*

I (Henrietta) grew up in Taipei city. There were many temples, big and small, near where I lived. In my home, we had a wooden altar standing against one side of the wall in the living room, where our ancestors' tablets and some statues of deities stood high. My mother burned incense and worshipped them every morning. On special occasions, such as the 1st day and the 15th day of each month on the lunar calendar, special rituals were practiced and offerings such as food, fruit, and cookies would be placed on the altar stand. My mother would ask the ancestors and gods to protect the family and make sure children were behaving and got good scores on every test. Apparently, the power of the home worship was not strong enough to correct my naughty behavior. My mother took me to a big temple nearby, Baoan Temple *bǎoān gōng* (保安宮) and asked the main god in the temple to take me in as his "god-daughter." After that, every year I had to go pay my respects at his birthday because he was my "god-father."

TAIWAN IS COMPACT BUT VARIED

Taiwan is a small island, fitting within the boundaries of the state of Indiana, but has almost twice the population of New Jersey with almost 24 million people.[2] It is roughly 394 kilometers (245 miles) long and 72 kilometers (90 miles) wide. Because of its compact size, it is easy to get around. In fact, even the most remote places on the island are not that far away. You can get to know Taiwan pretty well after a few months there. This is facilitated by Taiwan's excellent public transportation systems. There are world-class metro systems in the big cities and high-speed train systems throughout the west coast, as well as extensive bus lines. Driving or riding a scooter in Taiwan are also viable options.

For being such a small island, Taiwan has a remarkably diverse landscape. The east is dominated by mountains and gorges while the west is sloping plains. Because of this, the majority of the population lives on the north and west sides of the island. The west is also the industrial center of Taiwan where much of the manufacturing takes place. Taiwan's tallest mountain, Jade Mountain *yù shān* (玉山), is nearly 4,000 meters (13,000 feet) tall and receives snow in the winter. There are nine national parks in Taiwan, providing ample opportunities to get outside the cities and explore some beautiful mountains or beaches. In the south there are nice beaches with snorkeling, windsurfing, surfing, and other beach activities. The most famous beach area is Kenting National Park *kěndīng guójiā gōngyuán* (墾丁國家公園) on the island's southern tip. There are other beautiful areas with lakes and waterfalls as well.

This is not to say that all regions of Taiwan are the same culturally. Northern Taiwan has a different feel from southern Taiwan. The smaller towns on the east coast have a more laid-back vibe than the hustle and bustle in Taipei. Kaohsiung and other cities in the south have a distinctive feel, with many of the residents speaking Taiwanese as their dominant language. Not only is the language distinctive in the south, the food can vary as well.

HOW IS TAIWAN DIFFERENT FROM MAINLAND CHINA?

Taiwan has a different vibe than Mainland China. It feels more Western, more casual, and less strict. You do not have to walk around with your passport. You don't have to worry about being somewhere where foreigners are not supposed to be. For example, Taiwan does not have hotels that are off-limits to foreigners like in China, and you do not need to show your ID when you purchase train tickets. It is also easier to become a resident in Taiwan.

People in Taiwan tend to dress quite fashionably, even those with less income. Their behavior is welcoming to strangers; that is, they tend to be polite, to everyone, not just those within their inner group. There is less of an in-group/out-group distinction like there is in China. The streets of Taiwan feel safer. Though Mainland China is a very safe place compared to most countries with big cities, there is still quite a bit of petty theft, especially at places like train and bus stations where there are large crowds of people, and foreigners are particularly targeted. In Taiwan, this is much less the case. Of course crime exists, but we are much less worried about it in Taiwan than we are in China.

Things are quite clean in Taiwan. In China, buildings that were fairly recently built seem to age fairly quickly. This is likely due to less vigorous maintenance practices. In fact, it is not uncommon for public restrooms in buildings like a college campus to smell bad, and to not have any hand soap for washing up. It is also difficult to find trash cans in public places. Many areas of Chinese cities still have Soviet-style architecture that is drab, dirty, and not very nice looking. The Taiwanese are fastidious about hygiene, cleanliness, and order, and it is reflected even at the street level, where you will seldom see any litter. The streets are generally well lit and clean, and the traffic is orderly with most drivers obeying traffic laws. It is very safe being a pedestrian in Taiwan.

THE CHINESE LANGUAGE IN TAIWAN

Even though Mandarin Chinese is the official language of both Mainland China and Taiwan, Taiwan's Mandarin has some unique characteristics. Taiwan's Mandarin is influenced by the regional dialect spoken in Taiwan and across the straits in Fujian Province. The pronunciation is a bit different, there are some different grammatical structures, and vocabulary varies. If you speak any Chinese, you will notice these differences right away. One of the more noticeable differences is the Taiwan Mandarin tendency to pronounce certain initial sounds differently. For example, the standard Chinese way of saying "to know" is *zhidao*, with a hard "j" sound in the initial syllable. But in Taiwan it would be pronounced *zidao*, with a softer "dz" sound.

The biggest language difference is with the written language. Taiwan (as well as Hong Kong) uses traditional Chinese characters. This is the form of written characters that were used all over China for centuries. In the early 1950s, the Communist government simplified the writing system in an effort to ease the burden of literacy. Simplified Chinese characters are easier to learn and write, but people in Taiwan and Hong Kong will tell you that traditional characters are more aesthetically pleasing and reflect long-standing traditional values. There are enough similarities between traditional and simplified characters so that it is not too difficult to learn one after having learned the other, but it does take some effort. It is hard to make the case that literacy is easier with simplified characters when Taiwan and Hong Kong have higher literacy rates than Mainland China.

In recent decades Taiwan has also made great efforts to embrace their multilingual society. Many in Taiwan, like in Mainland China, speak other dialects of Chinese as their native language. The two main dialects spoken are Southern Min dialect *mǐnnán huà* (閩南話), also called Taiwanese *tái yǔ* (台語), and Hakka *kèjiā huà* (客家話). In the second half of the twentieth century, the Taiwan government promoted Mandarin as the national language and discouraged use of other dialects, but in recent decades there has been a push to not only recognize Taiwanese and Hakka, but also promote their use. In fact, in Taiwan today, when you ride the MTR (metro system) or trains, you will hear all announcements in Mandarin, Taiwanese, Hakka, and English.

STUDYING CHINESE IN TAIWAN

Taiwan's universities have been in the business of teaching Chinese as a foreign language for a long time. One of the two oldest, largest, and most well-known programs is National Taiwan Normal University's Mandarin Training Center (MTC), which was established in 1956 as a center for teaching Chinese to foreigners. It is the largest program in Taiwan, teaching approximately 1,700 students per year from about eighty different countries.[3] The other is National Taiwan University's International Chinese Language Program (ICLP), which was established in 1962 to cater to the needs of Stanford University students studying Chinese. It has since provided excellent Chinese language training to thousands of students from more than thirty countries. Many other Taiwan universities all over the island offer excellent Chinese language instruction for foreigners. Because of this long history of instruction of Chinese as a foreign language, Taiwan programs tend to have high-quality instruction and well-trained teachers (many having degrees and experience from Western universities), and are able to cater effectively to the needs of foreign students.

TAIWAN HAS A DIFFERENT VIBE

In Taiwan, I (Matt) feel a little less like an outsider, less like a foreigner. Part of that is because there are quite a few more foreigners (per capita) who live in Taiwan than in Mainland China. In fact, there are about the same number of foreigners living in Taiwan as in China (almost 800,000), and Taiwan is a much smaller place.[4] Keep in mind that the majority of foreigners in Taiwan are workers from various parts of Southeast Asia, Indonesia, Vietnam, Malaysia, the Philippines, and so on. For various reasons, such as increasing pollution and traffic in China's cities, and lack of personal freedoms, more foreigners are leaving Mainland China and relocating to other places, including Taiwan. This has been accelerated by Mainland China's strict zero COVID policy during the worldwide COVID-19 pandemic.

The people of Taiwan are also unbelievably kind and friendly. The term Taiwanese people use to describe their hospitality is *rénqíngwèi* (人情味). If you walk around the streets of any city in Taiwan and look even remotely confused, there is a high likelihood that someone will approach you and offer assistance. They are also incredibly honest and helpful. One day a student was using an ATM and inadvertently left his card in the machine and walked away. A few moments later he was chased down by the next customer in line, who had discovered his card and returned it. Anecdotes like this are what make Taiwan a desirable place to live. In other words, foreigners in Taiwan are often not treated as such. They are treated just like anyone else, with respect and kindness.

Even though the Taiwanese adhere closely to traditional Chinese values and ethics, they seem to have greater freedom of expression. This is reflected in the way they dress, the activities in which they engage, and how they interact with others. They seem less bound to group dynamics than many in China. This may be in part due to their exposure to outside influences, both Western and Asian. Western, Japanese, and Korean fashions are very popular in Taiwan, as is popular culture from these areas. Indeed, Taiwan is thoroughly modern in every way.

TAIWAN IS EASY FOR TRAVELERS AND STUDENTS

Taiwan is very accessible for foreigners, as it does not require a visa for North Americans and Europeans staying less than 90 days during normal years. However, Taiwan did require foreign students to apply for special-entry permits for staying fewer than 90 days during the COVID-19 pandemic.

It is easy to access money all over the island at just about any ATM machine. Most places accept cash, foreign credit cards, and even your local bank's debit cards. This eliminates the need to go to a bank and exchange money. You can also use a regular credit card just about anywhere, including hotels, shopping, buying train tickets, and so on. In Mainland China the only places we have been able to use a North American credit card is at large international hotels. You can't use foreign credit cards in many stores or restaurants, even at touristy places outside those tier-one cities (e.g., Beijing, Shanghai, Guangzhou). We thought this would change with time, but as of prior to the COVID-19 pandemic, this was still the case.

> In October 2019, I (Henrietta) traveled to Harbin, the capital of Heilongjiang Province in northeastern China, and stayed in the most famous hotel on Central Boulevard, which was the first *shèwài jiǔdiàn* (涉外酒店) in Harbin, a hotel designated specifically for foreigners. At check-out time, the hotel did not accept my Visa or American Express card because they were not issued by a Chinese bank. There were a dozen banks on Central Boulevard; however, none would allow me to do a currency exchange because I did not have a Chinese bank account with those banks. Eventually, I had to exchange money from a local friend and paid my hotel fees with cash.

China is increasingly moving to a cashless society, and it is becoming even more difficult for travelers, students, and tourists who do not have bank accounts in China or money in a WeChat account.

In 2019, I (Henrietta) visited a famous tea garden in Suzhou (Mainland China) with a friend. When it was time to pay, I did not have any credit in my WeChat account, and the teahouse did not accept cash or credit cards! They expected everyone to pay via Chinese apps that require links to bank accounts in China. After negotiating with the waitress for 30 minutes, she finally agreed to accept cash, but she had to go find change from somewhere else. In the end, it took me more than 40 minutes to pay a bill at a teahouse located at a famous and popular tourist location.

It is also nice when traveling in Taiwan that you do not always have to carry your passport with you. Traveling by train is straightforward—just show your ticket and you are off. You can stay just about anywhere in Taiwan. In China, some kinds of hotels—typically smaller, more inexpensive business-type hotels—are closed to foreigners. In some small cities or rural areas, only certain hotels are open to foreigners. In Taiwan, this is not the case. Airbnb and booking sites like Hotels.com work just fine in Taiwan, and foreigners are welcome to stay anywhere locals can stay.

Taiwan has a world-class universal health-care system. Residents are charged a very minimal amount for medical expenses with the government health-care system, and surprisingly, this applies to foreigners as well. We have heard many stories of foreigners injured or sick in Taiwan and showing up at a hospital to be treated well and not charged a penny. Medical care is modern, efficient, and well organized.

Foreigners are allowed to live just about anywhere they want. Though rent is not cheap in Taiwan's large cities, the cost of living is a bit lower than in China's big cities. Housing costs are rising considerably in China's big cities where most foreigners live, work, and study. That is easily the single most expensive part of living in Mainland China.

In the past, Taiwan, especially in the large urban areas like Taipei, have been more expensive than large cities in China. However, in recent years that gap is narrowing. The cost of living in big cities in China is rising rapidly, especially rent. Rental prices have gone up considerably in the 2000s, especially in large cities like Beijing, Shanghai, Nanjing, Guangzhou, and Shenzhen. The general consensus is that for working, you are likely to make more money in China, but Taiwan is more livable and has a more comfortable way of life.

To summarize, here is a short, quick list of things we like about Taiwan:

1. No visa is required for most foreigners staying fewer than 90 days during normal years.
2. No firewall; the media and internet are open with no restrictions.
3. Religion is an integral part of life in Taiwan.
4. It is cleaner, with a lot less pollution.
5. People in Taiwan are used to foreigners and are warmer toward them. You are not on display like you can be in China.
6. It is more orderly, from traffic to standing in lines.
7. There seems to be more traditional Chinese culture around, physically and in attitudes.

HIGHLIGHTS OF TAIWAN HISTORY

- Taiwan is inhabited by aboriginals of Austronesian descent for nearly 5,000 years before contact from the outside.
- 239 AD: First mention of contact with China. The Chinese emperor sends 10,000 Chinese troops to explore the island. At that time, it is not considered a part of China.
- 12th century: Small numbers of Chinese likely settled on Taiwan.
- 1430: Ming Dynasty (1368–1644) explorer Cheng Ho visits Taiwan and makes contact with the aboriginals. First time the name Taiwan is used.
- 1517: Portuguese sailors sail through Taiwan Strait and name the island Ilha Formosa, or "beautiful island."
- 1622: Dutch arrive in the area, gain control over the Pescadores, and set up a post on Taiwan.
- 1642: Dutch East India Company claim sovereignty of Taiwan for Holland.
- 1661: Dutch rule ends when defeated by Zhèng Chénggōng's (鄭成功, aka Koxinga) Chinese forces. He establishes a Ming-style government on Taiwan (independent of Mainland Chinese rule, which is governed by the Manchus of the Qing dynasty, 1644–1912).
- 1683: The Qing dynasty formally annexes Taiwan and rules until 1895.
- 1884: Beijing officially recognizes the political administration of Taiwan with Liú Míng-Chuán as governor.

- Until 1886, Taiwan is considered a part of Fujian Province.
- 1895: China defeated by Japan; Treaty of Shimonoseki cedes Taiwan to Japanese rule. Chinese on Taiwan claim independence and establish the short-lived Republic of Taiwan.
- 1895–1945: Taiwan is ruled as a colony of Japan.
- 1945: Nationalist forces are sent to Taiwan by the Kuomintang Party (KMT), and the Republic of China is reestablished. The Republic of China in Taiwan maintains UN and Western recognition as a legitimate Chinese government until 1979.
- 1947, February 28: The 228 Incident, or February 28 Incident, and the beginning of the "White Terror." An anti-government uprising demanding free elections and a clean government is violently suppressed by the KMT military and results in somewhere between 18,000 and 28,000 people killed. It marks the beginning of Taiwan's independence movement in the modern era.
- 1947–1987: White Terror period where all political dissent against the KMT is suppressed, often brutally. Many of Taiwan's intellectual and social elites are imprisoned or killed.
- 1949: End of the Chinese Civil War. Chiang Kai-shek and more than 1.5 million Chinese flee to Taiwan. Martial law is instituted in Taiwan, continuing until 1987. Chairman Mao never considered Taiwan a part of China.
- 1950: Beginning of the Korean War, when the United States reverses its hands-off policy toward the KMT.
- 1964: US aid to Taiwan is stopped.
- 1971: Taiwan is expelled from the United Nations, and the People's Republic of China (PRC) is recognized as the legitimate government of China. PRC takes over ROC's UN Security Council seat.
- 1978: Chiang Ching-kuo (son of Chiang Kai-shek) becomes president of the Republic of China.
- 1979: Pressured by the PRC, the United States cuts diplomatic ties with Taiwan.
- 1979: "Taiwan Relations Act" restores nearly official level of relations between Taiwan and the United States.
- 1979: The Kaohsiung Incident, where police killed pro-democracy protestors and arrested all opposition leaders. International attention is drawn to the KMT's oppressive regime.
- 1986: First democratic elections in Taiwan. The Democratic Progressive Party (DPP) won seats in the Legislative Yuan.

- 1987: Chiang Ching-kuo officially abolishes martial law and allows family visits to Mainland China.
- 1988: Chiang Ching-kuo of the KMT Party dies and vice president Lee Teng-hui becomes president, ending Mainland Chinese minorities' hold on political power in Taiwan, which ushers in a transition to majority, or Taiwanese, rule. He launches a "Taiwanization" program that relaxes restrictions on native language and culture.
- 1993: Taiwan and China hold preliminary talks to normalize relations.
- 1996: Lee Teng-hui is reelected to a new term.
- 2000, 2004: Chen Shui-bian of the DPP wins the presidential elections, the first time a non-KMT candidate presides over Taiwan. He announces that he would not declare independence for Taiwan as long as China does not attack.
- 2001: Taiwan lifts a fifty-year ban on trade and investment with China.
- 2002: Taiwan officially enters the World Trade Organization, a few weeks after China.
- 2005: First direct flights between Taiwan and Mainland China since 1949. First meeting since 1949 between KMT and Communist officials.
- 2008, 2012: Ma Ying-jeou of the KMT wins the presidential elections.
- 2008: President Ma apologizes for the imprisonment of tens of thousands of political dissidents during the 1950s and 1960s White Terror period.
- 2009: Leaders of Taiwan and China exchange direct messages for the first time in sixty years.
- 2010: Taiwan and China sign a free trade pact.
- 2012: China is Taiwan's biggest trading partner, worth $110 billion a year.
- 2014: Taiwan and China hold first government-to-government talks in Nanjing.
- 2015: President Ma Ying-jeou and China's President Xi Jinping hold talks in Singapore.
- 2016, 2020: Tsai Ing-wen of the DPP wins the presidential elections.
- 2017: Parliament votes to remove symbols of Taiwan's authoritarian past, including references to Chiang Kai-shek.

CURRENT STATE OF TAIWAN-CHINA RELATIONS, KNOWN AS CROSS-STRAIT RELATIONS

China believes Taiwan is a breakaway province that inevitably will be reunited with the Mainland and come under Chinese rule, either peacefully or by force. On the other hand, many Taiwanese feel that they already effectively have a separate nation. They have democratically elected officials, their own constitution, and an army of 300,000 soldiers. China has proposed a "one country, two systems" approach to Taiwan where it would be able to remain semi-autonomous from Chinese rule. However, most Taiwanese reject this possibility, with many looking to recent developments in Hong Kong and its new national security law.

There are basically three main schools of thought among Taiwanese about their relationship with Mainland China. The largest group by far favors continuing the status quo—that is, not moving toward true independence and thereby not provoking China, but also not in favor of reunification. The second group favors independence, a complete break with China, and no reunification with China. The third and smallest group favors reunification with China. Officially, the Kuomingtang Party (KMT) favors eventual reunification with China, and the Democratic Progressive Party (DPP) favors eventual independence.

The United States does not officially recognize Taiwan as a sovereign nation, but because of the Taiwan Relations Act, it affirms support for Taiwan including the sale of arms for defense and the possibility that the United States would support Taiwan if attacked. The US government refers to this situation as strategic ambiguity.

Beginning in 2018, Mainland China has insisted that international companies not refer to Taiwan as separate from China. China continues to put pressure on the United States, warning them not to interfere with Taiwanese affairs. This includes a Chinese ban on direct talks between US government officials and Taiwanese government officials. The United States has long supplied Taiwan with military weapons, and the current Biden administration has committed ongoing support, including defense measures for Taiwan.

Under President Xi Jinping's leadership, China has been increasingly aggressive toward Taiwan, often in the form of military exercises near Taiwan and strong rhetoric.

2

WHO LIVES IN TAIWAN?

To the casual observer, Taiwan seems like a very homogenous place where everyone is Chinese. Walking around the streets and public places, everyone seems to be speaking Chinese. While it is true that most are indeed ethnically Chinese, there are several different ways that people in Taiwan identify themselves and others, and it is important to understand this in order to avoid misunderstandings or giving offense. Language and accent are core identifiers among those living in Taiwan and often shape a person's identity.

A night market in Taiwan. *Image courtesy of Matthew B. Christensen*

A neighborhood temple. *Image courtesy of Matthew B. Christensen*

In Taiwan, a small island with an area of 35,809 square kilometers (13,826 square miles) on the main island (about the size of the state of Indiana),[1] you can find native speakers of at least twenty different languages among the 23.33 million citizens.[2] This is due to its complicated history over the past 400 years. It is not an easy task to define the identity of the residents on the island. It truly depends on whom you ask and when. The answers you receive will likely vary.

The languages spoken on the island include sixteen Austronesian languages used by sixteen distinct aboriginal tribes recognized by Taiwan's current government,[3] the Southern Min language *mǐnnán huà* (閩南話), also called Taiwanese *tái yǔ* (台語, literally "Taiwan language"), Hakka *kèjiā huà* (客家話), Mandarin Chinese, and Vietnamese. Many terms have been used to identify residents on the island who speak these languages. They consist of the following:

- Taiwanese aboriginals *yuánzhù mín* (原住民, literally "original residents")
- Hakka *kèjiā rén* (客家人, literally "guest people")

- Taiwanese *táiwān rén* (台灣人, literally "Taiwan people") or *běnshěng rén* (本省人, literally "people of *this* province")
- Mainlanders *wàishěng rén* (外省人, literally "people from *outside* the province")
- Chinese *zhōngguó rén* (中國人, "Chinese ethnic people")
- Mainlanders *dàlù rén* (大陸人, "people from Mainland China")
- New immigrants *xīnzhù mín* (新住民, literally "new residents")

Below, we approach this complex identity issue of Taiwan's residents by describing who uses which language(s) and how those users identify themselves, primarily following the timeline of Taiwan's history over the past 400 years (see the "Highlights of Taiwan History" at the end of chapter 1).

TAIWANESE ABORIGINALS AND AUSTRONESIAN LANGUAGES

Many different Austronesian tribes resided all over the island for thousands of years before outsiders (Han Chinese, Dutch, Spanish, and Portuguese) arrived in Taiwan. When outsiders arrived, they called those tribes living in the mountainous regions *gāoshān zú* (高山族), which literally means "high mountain tribes," and those on the flat coastal plains or valleys *píngpǔ zú* (平埔族), which means "flatlands tribes."[4] Each tribe possessed its own unique language, traditional customs, rituals, and special tribal clothing. It is not difficult to distinguish true aboriginals from Han people based on their appearance, because aboriginals normally have more distinctive facial features and darker skin tones, while the facial features of Han people are generally not as prominent.

During the Dutch invasion period (1624–1662), it was estimated there were forty-five diverse tribes spread out on the island. As a consequence of several centuries of intermarriage with outsiders, mainly with Han people from the southeast coastal provinces of Mainland China (Fujian and Guangdong), only eighteen of those tribes could be identified by the early nineteenth century.[5] Geographically, it was much easier for outsiders to access the areas where the flatlands tribes resided. As a result, these tribes underwent serious cultural assimilation with the Han people, much more than those residing in mountainous regions. After the Japanese arrived on the island in the late nineteenth century as the new colonists, they were interested in the natural resources in Taiwan's mountain regions. Subsequently, the Japanese invaded the villages of many mountain tribes. Once a tribal territory was forced to open up, cultural assimilation was inevitable.

The aboriginals encountered tremendous economic disadvantages after outsiders invaded their homelands, and they were discriminated against by outsiders as "uncultivated" or "primitive."

> I (Henrietta) grew up in Taiwan during the 1970s and 1980s. During that period of time, derogatory terms like *shāndì rén* (山地人 "mountain area people") and *fān zǎi* (番仔) or *fān rén* (番人), which literally means "uncultivated" or "primitive" people, were used to refer to Taiwanese aboriginals.

Beginning in the 1990s, Taiwan gradually transitioned to a democratic political system, and Taiwanese began to recognize and embrace their multicultural and multilingual society, including aboriginals and their cultures. Those derogatory terms used to refer to aboriginals were discouraged and deemed disrespectful. A neutral term, *yuánzhù mín* (原住民, literally "original residents"), was promoted and used in all official documents in 1994.[6] Moreover, the Taiwan government instituted a series of preferential treatments to make sure Taiwanese aboriginals receive compensation, participation, and representation. For instance, when Taiwanese aboriginals participate in various college entrance examinations, they receive extra bonuses to boost their total scores. Furthermore, when competing for funds to study abroad, aboriginal students can take advantage of quotas reserved for them. Moreover, to make sure aboriginals have proper representation in the Taiwanese congress, a certain number of seats are reserved for aboriginal representatives.

Many young aboriginals whose dominant language is now Mandarin Chinese, the official language on the island, can no longer speak their native tribal languages, though they are still closely associated with their own cultures. Language loss has become a serious issue among them. In recent years, younger generations of aboriginals have been willing to return to their own tribes, and want to not only preserve their cultures and languages but also make them known to outsiders. In 1994, the Shung Ye Museum of Formosan Aborigines opened in Taipei.[7] It focuses on information about the essence of aboriginal cultures, including their artifacts, costumes, and ritual items, which help outsiders understand their unique cultures and values. The museum also offers many educational activities to students and schoolteachers in order to enhance their knowledge about Taiwan's unique aboriginal tribes.

OUTSIDERS

In addition to Taiwanese aboriginals, most citizens on the island are the descendants of Han Chinese people who migrated from Mainland China during the Ming (1368–1644) and Qing (1644–1912) dynasties, as well as during the post–World War II period from 1945 to 1949. These Han people brought with them their own languages and cultures. During the Ming and Qing dynasties, the majority of Han people migrating to Taiwan were from Fujian Province on the southeastern coast of China, which is only 180 kilometers (110 miles) across the Taiwan Strait. They mainly spoke Southern Min and Hakka.

Those arriving in Taiwan between 1945 and 1949 were from many different parts of Mainland China and spoke their own local languages. (Because these varieties are not mutually intelligible, we consider them different languages, not dialects, even though they share the same writing system.) However, the majority of them could speak Mandarin Chinese, though with a wide range of different accents.

HAKKA *KÈJIĀ RÉN* (客家人) AND THEIR LANGUAGE

One group of Han people from Mainland China who migrated to Taiwan during the Ming and Qing dynasties spoke Hakka. This group is called *kèjiā rén* (客家人), literally "guest people." Normally, one cannot distinguish native speakers of Hakka from those of Taiwanese until they speak. According to a survey done in 2021, published by the Hakka Affairs Council in Taiwan, the population of Hakka on the island was 19.8 percent, an increase of 0.5 percent from 2016, which could be a sign of the rise of identity recognition by the Hakka. However, the population who were able to speak Hakka decreased from 46.8 percent in 2016 to 38.3 percent in 2021.[8] Like aboriginals in Taiwan, language loss among the younger generations of Hakka in Taiwan is serious, mainly caused by the so-called National Language Policy implemented by the Japanese colonists from 1895 to 1945, and by Chiang Kai-shek's regime from 1947 to 1987. During those two periods, Japanese and Mandarin Chinese, respectively, were the only official languages and any other varieties of local languages were suppressed. The social status and the economic advantages associated with the official languages, and the social stigma related to local languages discouraged young generations who spoke local languages to learn and use their mother tongues.

I (Henrietta) still remember clearly that a teacher of mine in elementary school in the late 1970s used a stick to slap the palms of my hands when I was caught unintentionally speaking my mother tongue, Taiwanese *mǐnnán huà* (閩南話). During the 1970s and 1980s, anyone who was caught speaking non-Mandarin Chinese under the National Language Policy would be punished physically or be fined at school.

TAIWANESE *TÁIWĀN RÉN* (台灣人) AND SOUTHERN MIN LANGUAGE *MǏNNÁN HUÀ* (閩南話)

In 1662, Zhèng Chénggōng (鄭成功), a Chinese Ming loyalist, and his troops defeated the Dutch colonists in Taiwan. He and his successors were mostly from the southeastern coast of Mainland China and spoke Southern Min. They established Han culture as the societal foundation on the island until Taiwan was ceded to Japan as part of the Treaty of Shimonoseki in 1895. The most significant element that was instituted and still affects many Taiwanese people's morals and values to the present day is conservative Confucianism. Some basic Confucian principles include filial piety, group identity, importance of education, and social propriety. For foreigners who plan to study or work in Taiwan, having a good understanding of these Confucian principles and how they are practiced in Taiwanese people's daily lives will help them comprehend why Taiwanese do things in a particular way. Examples will be given in the following chapters where we discuss aspects of living, studying, and working in Taiwan.

In Taiwan today, about 72 percent of the population are native speakers of Southern Min, but also speak Mandarin Chinese, though with a range of Taiwanese accents, from light to heavy.[9] A higher percentage of the population in southern Taiwan speaks Taiwanese than in the north. Similar to many younger generations of native speakers of Hakka, younger generations of native speakers of Taiwanese nowadays are not able to speak the language as fluently as their parents because Mandarin Chinese has become their dominant language. Nevertheless, most of them have a passive knowledge of the language and can understand it with no problem.

The term "Taiwan people," *táiwān rén* (台灣人), has certain nuances of meaning to different people. It truly depends on whom you ask and when. Not only do these people, whose native language is Southern Min, identify themselves as "Taiwan people," but some other residents on the island whose native languages are not Southern Min also identify this way.

Who Lives in Taiwan? 23

A *táiwān rén* (台灣人) might also consider themself as *běnshěng rén* (本省人, literally "people of *this* province") or *wàishěng rén* (外省人, literally "people from *outside* the province"), or even *zhōngguó rén* (中國人) or *dàlù rén* (大陸人). The identity issue is complicated on the island, and the categories mentioned here are not mutually exclusive.

BĚNSHĚNG RÉN (本省人) VS. *WÀISHĚNG RÉN* (外省人)

The term *wàishěng rén* (外省人) is used by local residents on the island to refer to those people from Mainland China who arrived in Taiwan at the end of World War II in 1945. At that time the Japanese surrendered their rule over Taiwan to the Kuomintang Party (KMT) of the Republic of China (ROC). The ROC was founded in Mainland China in 1912, and was under the leadership of Chiang Kai-shek when Japan ended its colonial control of the island. In 1945, some residents on the island were very much looking forward to reuniting with their motherland *zǔguó* (祖國) after five decades of Japanese rule, and enthusiastically considered the island as a province: Taiwan Province *táiwān shěng* (台灣省). This implied Taiwan was one of the governmental provinces of the ROC. Even in the 1970s and 1980s, the concept of Taiwan as a province was still prevalent, and that could be seen by how Taiwanese wrote their addresses. Before I (Henrietta) moved to the United States in the 1990s, the way I wrote my address on the envelope always began with the following: 台灣省台北市延平北路, which means Taiwan Province Taipei City Yanping North Road.

At that time, the people on the island called themselves *táiwān rén* (台灣人) or *běnshěng rén* (本省人). The notion of being *běnshěng rén* (本省人) was based on the idea of identifying themselves as citizens of the Republic of China, *zhōnghuá mínguó* (中華民國), and living in a particular province. That is why there is a distinction between people of *this* province (*běnshěng rén* 本省人) vs. people coming from *outside* of this province (*wàishěng rén* 外省人). No matter which province they were from, they were all considered citizens of the Republic of China.

In October 1945, the KMT government officially arrived in Taiwan to take over administrative control of the island from the Japanese. The residents of Taiwan lined up to welcome the authorities from their "motherland" but were stunned and bewildered by what they saw. I (Henrietta) am fortunate to have met Mrs. June Huang, who witnessed the transition in 1945 in Taiwan, and is currently living in Southern California with her four children. Mrs. Huang grew up in Taiwan and lived there from the 1930s to

1960s. She graciously agreed to have an interview with me. She described what she saw when the KMT authorities arrived in Taiwan in 1945:[10]

> Many residents waited in lines to welcome the new ruling authorities from the motherland. When the military personnel arrived, they were in shabby uniforms and were wearing shoes made from straw. Their manners were not civilized. It was a huge contrast to Japanese military and government officials, who always dressed up neatly and were disciplined on the island. Local residents were just confused. People could not comprehend how a disorderly group like that could defeat a well-organized, advanced country like Japan.

When I asked Mrs. Huang what she thought of the Japanese while they were in Taiwan, she said:

> When new colonists arrived, there would be inevitable resistance from the local inhabitants, and conflicts between two sides were there. Overall, Japanese did contribute a great deal to the island. Taiwan was built by the Japanese. They improved Taiwanese people's life quality by constructing railroads throughout the island, expanding ports for import and export, improving the medical system on the island, and installing running water in homes. After the Japanese arrived in 1895, they realized Taiwan had a serious water problem. Residents did not have access to clean water in their houses, so people got sick easily and frequently. Outside the home, flooding was a common disaster when Taiwanese relied heavily on agriculture production. Therefore, the Japanese began water treatment, constructing waterways, installing running water to houses, building dams to control heavy rain. When the KMT troops arrived, they were surprised by how advanced and orderly Taiwan was. When they saw running water at Taiwanese people's home, they were amazed because they had never seen it before!

Like any military organization during a war, the quality and behavior of individual soldiers can vary considerably. The majority of KMT troops whom local Taiwanese residents encountered in 1945 were mostly uneducated, and their conduct was often corrupt and unjustified. This is not to say there were no well-educated Chinese elites who migrated to Taiwan during that period of time.

What Mrs. Huang described was the constructive side of Japanese rule that some residents on the island experienced, though she also acknowledged that there were conflicts between Japanese and local residents. Numerous historical documents reveal that many events that happened under Japanese colonial rule were exploitative, brutal, and inhumane against Taiwanese and aboriginals who exhibited any resistance to the Japanese. However, we believe it is important to hear from non-historians as well. Their experiences and attitudes toward the Japanese might explain why, up to this day, Taiwanese still strongly embrace Japanese culture.

CHINESE ZHŌNGGUÓ RÉN (中國人) OR TAIWANESE TÁIWĀN RÉN (台灣人)

In 1946, the KMT authorities began to implement the so-called National Language *guó yǔ* (國語) Policy and designated Mandarin Chinese as the only "civilized" language that was allowed in public and at home. Any other varieties of communication like Taiwanese and Hakka were forcefully suppressed and labeled as "primitive" local dialects. Gradually, the new ruling authorities lost respect, and tension between local residents and newly arrived Mainlanders increased drastically. Eventually, it led to an uprising throughout the island. Unfortunately, the anti-government uprising was brutally suppressed by the KMT forces, which killed thousands of Taiwanese, estimated between 18,000 and 28,000, beginning on February 28, 1947. This became known as the 228 Incident.[11] The 228 Incident marked the start of four decades of the White Terror, and the island was placed under martial law in 1949. Many Taiwanese elites were massacred during this period, and the wish of reuniting with the "motherland" was shattered. Since the 228 Incident, a movement to push for Taiwan independence took off and has continued to this day.

The 228 Incident was a clear defining point for Taiwanese identity. Even though Chiang Kai-shek declared in 1949 that Taipei, Taiwan, was the temporary capital of the ROC and proclaimed sovereignty over all "China" including Mainland China, Taiwan, Outer Mongolia, and other areas, Taiwanese people did not want to be identified as *zhōngguó rén* (中國人) anymore. The idea of identifying themselves as Taiwanese *táiwān rén* (台灣人) gradually expanded among the residents on the island.

In 1949, more than 1 million Mainlanders fled from Mainland China to Taiwan. They, along with those who had arrived between 1945 and 1949, considered themselves Chinese *zhōngguó rén* (中國人), which referred to citizens of the Republic of China (ROC, aka Taiwan) *zhōnghuá mínguó* (中華民國), not the People's Republic of China (PRC, aka China) *zhōnghuá rénmín gònghéguó* (中华人民共和国), which did not exist yet. Notice that the short form for the residents of the PRC is also Chinese *zhōngguó rén* (中國人), which is semantically ambiguous.

When I asked Mrs. Huang how she would identify herself before she moved to the United States in the late 1960s, without thinking, she responded immediately with: Taiwanese *táiwān rén* (台灣人). Many of my close friends' parents were *wàishěng rén* (外省人), migrating to Taiwan from Mainland China in 1949. They mostly considered themselves Chinese *zhōngguó rén* (中國人) or Mainlander *dàlù rén* (大陸人) because they were born and raised in Mainland China. Note that the term Chinese *zhōngguó rén* (中國人), which they used, refers to citizens of the Republic of China *zhōnghuá mínguó* (中華民國), not the People's Republic of China. Many of my friends are the second generation of those Mainlanders and often suffered identity crises as their family identity was different from most people they interacted with. Unlike native speakers of Taiwanese, they speak standard Mandarin Chinese without Taiwanese accents. As soon as they speak Mandarin Chinese, people know they are from a family of Mainlanders *wàishěng rén* (外省人).

In 2020, I (Henrietta) talked to two of my close friends, one female and one male, about their identity issues. The male friend, Mr. Chu, said that he considered himself "Chinese in Taiwan," *zài táiwān de zhōngguó rén* (在台灣的中國人) or *zài táiwān de dàlù rén* (在台灣的大陸人) because his parents were both from Mainland China, but he was born in Taiwan.[12] He further explained his definition of *zhōngguó* (中國) when he said he himself is "Chinese in Taiwan." He said he used China *zhōngguó* (中國) in a broader sense of Chinese ethnic people *zhōnghuá mínzú* (中華民族). He confessed that oftentimes he had a sense of identity crisis and felt he was an outsider during many stages of his life. Before he graduated from university in Taiwan, he was often called "*wàishěng rén*" (外省人), which implied "outsider." When he studied in the United States and later worked in Singapore, he was still an "outsider" to people in those two countries because he was not an American, nor was he a Singaporean. Then he worked in Suzhou, China. To the local residents in China, he was a Taiwanese *táiwān rén* (台灣人), which again suggests "outsider." When I asked him what his two college-age daughters think about their identities, he said, "Nowadays, under the 'green education' in Taiwan, the young generation all think they are Taiwanese *táiwān rén* (台灣人); so do my daughters. They do not think like me. They do not consider themselves Chinese *zhōngguó rén* (中國人) at all."

The term "green education" that Mr. Chu used refers to the influence of the Democratic Progressive Party (DPP), a Taiwanese nationalist and liberal political party in Taiwan, which won the presidency of Taiwan in the years 2000–2008 and 2016–present (2023). The complexity of Taiwanese identity issues is clearly manifest in Mr. Chu's family. Three generations all live in Taiwan and speak Mandarin Chinese as their dominant language, though with various degrees of different accents. However, they identify themselves distinctively, ranging from absolute Chinese *zhōngguó rén* (中國人) or Mainlanders *dàlù rén* (大陸人) to outright Taiwanese *táiwān rén* (台灣人) in less than seventy years.

I also interviewed a close female friend, Ms. Wang, about her identity issue.[13] Her father was also from Mainland China in 1949, but her mother was Taiwanese. She said her father considered himself Chinese *zhōngguó rén* (中國人) or Mainlander *dàlù rén* (大陸人), and she herself was often labeled as *wàishěng rén* (外省人). When I asked her how she defined her own identity despite how other people think of her, she said she considered herself Taiwanese *táiwān rén* (台灣人) because she was born and raised in Taiwan. She further clarified that her definition of being a Taiwanese did not mean she supported Taiwan's independence. She said she still thought of herself as a citizen of the Republic of China *zhōnghuá mínguó* (中華民國), not the People's Republic of China. After some discussion, she stated that the term "Chinese in/from Taiwan *zài táiwān de zhōngguó rén*" (在台灣的中國人), which was identical to the term that Mr. Chu used, was more appropriate to her thinking.

The identity shift among Taiwan citizens has been significant in the past three decades. In a poll released by the Taiwan Public Opinion Foundation (TPOF, 台灣民意基金會) in the early 1990s, only 26 percent of the residents on the island identified themselves as Taiwanese *táiwān rén* (台灣人), while around 33 percent of residents considered themselves both Taiwanese *táiwān rén* (台灣人) and Chinese *zhōngguó rén* (中國人), and another 33 percent Chinese *zhōngguó rén* (中國人). However, according to the TPOF, in April 2022, 80.1 percent of Taiwan citizens considered themselves Taiwanese, while only 5.3 percent considered themselves Chinese, and 10.2 percent considered themselves both Taiwanese and Chinese. In just thirty years, the number of people identifying themselves as Taiwanese rose more than 50 percent.[14]

INSIDERS VS. OUTSIDERS

During the 1970s and 1980s, the tension between *běnshěng rén* (本省人) and *wàishěng rén* (外省人) was still quite severe. *Wàishěng rén* (外省人) were considered outsiders but had control of the government and resources on the island. Most, if not all, were affiliated with the KMT, while the majority of *běnshěng rén* (本省人) were not. The tension affected many Taiwanese families, even in my own family.

> Before I (Henrietta) left Taiwan to study in the United States in the 1990s, my father often "reminded" me not to pick a *wàishěng rén* (外省人) to marry in the future, though he did not ban me from making friends with them. In my father's view, *wàishěng rén* (外省人) were outsiders, who could not speak our language, Taiwanese. During that time, I felt he was more worried that one day I would move to Mainland China if I were to marry a *wàishěng rén* (外省人), because that was where they were from and where they might return in the future.

Being identified as an "insider" in Taiwan means that you might get a good deal when shopping in traditional markets or night markets where Taiwanese is the dominant language.

> I (Henrietta) have been teaching Mandarin Chinese in the United States since 2000 as a graduate assistant, then as a full-time instructor since 2005. Being a language instructor, I had to be careful about my pronunciation, especially when I taught students at novice levels. As a result, I lost a great deal of my Taiwanese accent when I spoke Mandarin Chinese. During the past twenty years, when I returned to Taiwan to visit, I was often taken as *wàishěng rén* (外省人) or *dàlù rén* (大陸人) when I spoke Mandarin Chinese! The difference between being a *wàishěng rén* (外省人) and being a *dàlù rén* (大陸人) in Taiwan over the past twenty years is that the former is a resident of Taiwan, but the latter could just be a tourist from China, a "true outsider." Being identified as *wàishěng rén* (外省人) or *dàlù rén* (大陸人) means that I might not get a good deal when I shop in traditional markets or night markets, such as more generous servings or small discounts that "insiders" (*běnshěng rén* 本省人) would get. Therefore, whenever I visited traditional markets or a night market, I only spoke Taiwanese to "blend in."
>
> Another time when I was conscious about my identity and wanted to be perceived as an "insider" was whenever I took a taxi before GPS or Uber was widely used in Taiwan. During those times, I wanted to let the taxi drivers think I was a local and knew the routes even though my memory of some areas was already vague. I would only speak Taiwanese to taxi drivers to let them know that I was from there and I was a *běnshěng rén* (本省人), so they would not detour without my permission.

In short, the identity issue in Taiwan is a complicated one. It truly depends on whom you ask and when. People might consider themselves both Chinese *zhōngguó rén* (中國人) and Taiwanese *táiwān rén* (台灣人). My sister always thought of herself as Taiwanese *táiwān rén* (台灣人) until eight years ago. She now considers herself Chinese *zhōngguó rén* (中國人), after she switched from the PPT to the KMT political party.

NEW RESIDENTS *XĪNZHÙ MÍN* (新住民) AND THEIR LANGUAGES

New Residents *xīnzhù mín* (新住民) is a relatively new term, mainly applying to immigrants who live in Taiwan and have gained citizenship. In most cases, those New Residents settled in Taiwan through marriages with citizens of Taiwan. According to statistics released by Taiwan's Ministry of the Interior National Immigration Agency in April 2023, the biggest ethnic group that married citizens of Taiwan was people from Mainland China (61.32 percent).[15] After martial law was lifted in 1987, many collaborations and communication between people of Mainland China (PRC) and those from Taiwan (ROC) took place. For example, many Taiwanese factories were relocated from Taiwan to China for cheaper labor. Once contact between the two sides of the Taiwan Strait gained traction, chances for citizens from both sides to get married became higher. People in China share the same language, Mandarin Chinese, and a similar culture with Taiwanese, which makes these unions easier.

According to the same statistics, the second-largest group of New Residents is from Vietnam (19.55 percent), whose language and culture are distinct from Taiwanese language and culture. From 1987 to 2016, there were 93,617 Vietnamese citizens, who married into Taiwan. Among those, 92,974 were female, and only 643 were male. That is the reason why the terms used to refer to those Vietnamese immigrants focused on female residents in the beginning. The first term, Vietnamese brides *yuènán xīnniáng* (越南新娘), carries a negative connotation. Later, it was changed to Females of New Immigrants *xīnyímín nǚxìng* (新移民女性), then to Taiwan New Resident *táiwán xīnzhùmín* (台灣新住民).

There are other nationalities that have migrated to Taiwan, and they are also called Taiwan New Residents, such as Indonesians (5.41 percent), Hong Kong and Macao (3.63 percent), Filipinos (1.90 percent), and Thai (1.69 percent). Those immigrants bring with them their unique cultures and languages, which greatly enriches Taiwan's democratic society and food culture.

In 1987, Taiwan's martial law was lifted, and Taiwan began transitioning into a legitimate democratic political system. The National Language

Policy also underwent a transformation. In the early 1990s, the rise of localization or nativism *běntǔhuà yùndòng* (本土化運動) made it possible to broadcast native languages such as Hakka, Taiwanese, and aboriginal languages on TV and radio programs. Gradually, the National Language Policy began to recognize Taiwan's local languages in a positive way. For example, in 1996, the Taiwan government began implementing the Mother Tongue Policy *mǔyǔ zhèngcè* (母語政策). Under this policy, third through sixth graders were required to have 1 hour per week to learn about their mother tongues. In 2018, a revised language policy for elementary students was initiated, which made local languages (including Hakka, Taiwanese, and aboriginal languages) and languages of New Residents (such as Thai, Vietnamese, and Indonesian) possible elective courses.[16]

Taiwan may be small, but the complexity of Taiwanese identity and the varieties of languages spoken on the island are extraordinary. For foreigners who plan to study or work on the island, knowing how the local residents identify themselves will help avoid some awkward moments. The majority of residents on the island speak Mandarin Chinese like the people in Mainland China, though with different accents. However, just because they share the same language, by calling them Chinese *zhōngguó rén* (中國人) or Mainlanders *dàlù rén* (大陸人), you might unknowingly offend people, though they might not overtly display their feelings toward that comment.

Learning Mandarin Chinese, with some Taiwanese characteristics, will enable an outsider to more fully integrate into Taiwanese society and be trusted by locals. For example, dropping the *er* suffixes commonly used in northern Mainland Chinese will indicate that you are a sophisticated learner of Chinese and understand local conditions. It doesn't mean that you have to fully adopt a Taiwanese accent, but speaking standard Mandarin—without too much influence from other dialects—will be appreciated. Furthermore, learning some simple phrases in Taiwanese *tái yǔ* (台語) will go a long way toward ingratiating yourself with the locals. However, use caution with whom you try this, as there are many Taiwanese who do not speak *tái yǔ*. Westerners who speak fluent *tái yǔ* are rare, but those who can are widely respected and accepted.

FITTING IN AS A FOREIGNER IN TAIWAN

The Chinese have an idiom, *rùxiāng suísú* (入鄉隨俗), literally meaning "enter the countryside, follow the customs." It's the equivalent of the saying "when in Rome, do as the Romans do." To be successful in Taiwan, it is important to fit it, and by fitting in, we mean acting, speaking, and behaving as the Taiwanese would expect of someone. In other words, the Taiwanese should not have to modify their behavior to get along with you. You should modify your behavior so they are comfortable with you. You will always be a foreigner, but you should act in ways that the Taiwanese find normal and comfortable. No matter what your purpose is in going to Taiwan, to be successful, you need to be able to establish relationships with people, and in order to do that, people need to like you and want to spend time with you.

There is a phenomenon known as the "ugly American syndrome," and it goes something like this: Americans abroad seldom speak the language, assume everyone loves Americans and American culture, desperately want everyone to love them, and want everyone to know they are there. This often is manifested in Americans going around being loud and sometimes obnoxious. If you are reading this book, this probably does not apply to you. But be aware that if your goal in Taiwan is to establish meaningful and lasting relationships with the Taiwanese, then blending in is your best strategy. Below we provide some tips on how best to blend in and get along with the Taiwanese.

- *Learn some Chinese and/or Taiwanese.* Even if it's just a few polite phrases, this sends the signal that you care and want to learn more about them.
- *Eat local.* Don't always eat and hang out at Western food places. Go out to eat with your Taiwanese friends and colleagues.
- *Make friends.* Make friends, hang out with locals, socialize with your work colleagues. Eat lunch with them.
- *Dress the part.* Whether you are a student, doing an internship, or working, it is important that you dress appropriately for the occasion. If in doubt, observe how others are dressed and follow suit. Dress standards may be different from where you come from.
- *Keep your voice down.* Most Taiwanese tend to be a bit more subdued than many North Americans.
- *Avoid common stereotypes.* Not all Taiwanese are good at math and science, or are martial arts experts.
- *Learn about the culture.* Familiarize yourself with some basic Taiwan history, traditional Chinese religions and philosophy, and so on.
- *Be a keen observer.* If you are in a situation and don't know what to do, pause and observe what others are doing. Then follow suit.

- *Be polite, humble, and gracious.* The Taiwanese appreciate someone who knows the customs and is polite. Remember that you are the guest, so be appreciative of any help you receive. The Taiwanese value humility, so don't brag and talk constantly about yourself.

CULTURE SHOCK AND DEALING WITH CHANGE

Culture shock is when you experience feelings of disorientation or discomfort when confronting a new culture and different ways of doing things. It can be literally debilitating. Most everyone gets culture shock to some degree. I (Matt) have been traveling to China, Taiwan, and Hong Kong for thirty-five years and I still experience culture shock to some degree just about every time I go back. It's normal, but understanding what is happening can help you minimize the shock and allow you to more quickly adjust to your new situation.

Culture shock has four stages or phases: the honeymoon stage, the negotiation stage, the adjustment stage, and the mastery stage. Each of these stages may last from a day or two to up to a month or two.

The Honeymoon Stage

This stage occurs when you first arrive and everything seems new, interesting, maybe exotic and fun. You are dazzled by the new culture and everything around you. You may feel excited, energized, and enthusiastic. This stage may last a few days, weeks, or maybe a month. Like all honeymoons, this stage will come to an end.

The Negotiation Stage

This is when reality sets in, and things maybe aren't quite as bright and wonderful as they first seemed. You are realizing that things really are different. You may be having a hard time adjusting to the new food, the weather, the language, a new social situation, work practices, and so on. You might be feeling homesick, maybe a bit overwhelmed, maybe wondering what you have gotten yourself into. You are without your usual support network of family and friends. This stage can be quite stressful.

The Adjustment Stage

This is when you come to terms with your new life. You have made some adjustments and are getting into a rhythm, have made some friends, are getting along with your colleagues, and are better understanding not just what is different but why people are doing things the way they are. You are seeing things with new eyes and are able to adapt to your new situation. What may have seemed exotic or strange now seems normal, and you are okay with that. This stage may come along a month or two after arrival, but it may take up to a few months to get to this point.

The Mastery Stage

This is when you are able to fully integrate with society and get along well with others. You know what to expect, how to get things done, and how to interact smoothly. The more you understand about Chinese/Taiwanese culture and the language, the sooner you will get to this stage.

Minimizing Culture Shock

Many of the tips above about fitting in will help minimize your culture shock. The worst thing you can do is isolate yourself and avoid contact with others. Go with an open mind. Understand that things will be different—not inferior, just different. Try to acclimate to the new time zone as soon as possible. Get the rest you need but force yourself to stay up when you might normally be sleeping. Make sure to eat well. You may need to ease into some local food. In Taiwan it is easy to find familiar food, even at convenience stores. Take care of your mental health. Before you go, have a plan to deal with stress, anxiety, and depression. Work out what you will do if you are feeling down. Maybe it is a phone call to a family member or good friend. It might be escaping into a movie or TV show, or eating a favorite food. Make sure you have access to any medications you may need.

Table 2.1. Useful Phrases

Taiwanese (people)	*táiwān rén* (台灣人) or *běnshěng rén* (本省人)
Taiwanese (language)	*tái yǔ* (台語)
Chinese (people)	*zhōngguó rén* (中國人)
Chinese (language)	*zhōngwén* (中文) or *huá yǔ* (華語)
Mainlander	*dàlù rén* (大陸人) or *wàishěng rén* (外省人)
Southern Min language	*mǐnnán huà* (閩南話)
Hakka (people)	*kèjiā rén* (客家人)
Hakka (language)	*kèjiā huà* (客家話)
Taiwanese aboriginal	*yuánzhù mín* (原住民)
New immigrant	*xīnzhù mín* (新住民)
National Language	*guó yǔ* (國語), term used in Taiwan and Hong Kong to refer to standard Mandarin
Republic of China (ROC, aka Taiwan)	*zhōnghuá mínguó* (中華民國)
People's Republic of China (PRC, aka China)	*zhōnghuá rénmín gònghéguó* (中华人民共和国)
Chinese Ethnic People	*zhōnghúa mínzú* (中華民族)

3

GETTING AROUND IN TAIWAN

On a recent trip to Taiwan, I (Matt) flew in from Nanjing, on the Mainland. Taoyuan International Airport is modern, efficient, clean, and orderly. After passing through customs I headed to the taxi stand, waited a few minutes, then hopped into a taxi and rode a short distance to the Taoyuan High Speed Rail station. I had booked a ticket online for the High Speed Rail (HSR, Taiwan's bullet trains) to Chiayi where I was meeting a friend and colleague. At the train station I showed the agent at the ticket counter my email confirmation and within a couple minutes had my boarding pass in hand. In Chiayi I jumped into another taxi that took me to my hotel. Overall it was a remarkably smooth trip with quick and easy transfers. I was impressed with the excellent transportation infrastructure.

Taiwan is a relatively small island, roughly 394 kilometers (245 miles) long and 72 kilometers (45 miles) wide. With excellent infrastructure and a world-class transportation system, it is easy to get just about anywhere on the island quickly and conveniently. The system allows residents or travelers smooth access to all the metropolitan areas via train, and just about anywhere else by bus, car, scooter, or bicycle. In a relatively short time you could theoretically visit just about every part of the island, from the mountains to the beaches and all the big cities and villages in between.

Because of Taiwan's open and free society, traveling is relatively carefree. There are no restrictions on foreigners, no luggage scan at the entrance of train stations or MRT (Mass Rapid Transit *jiéyùn* 捷運), and no need to show your passport when boarding trains or other kinds of transport; foreigners are treated just like anyone else. You are free to travel anywhere anyone else can travel and can stay anywhere locals stay.

Even though Taiwan's cities are large and crowded, they can be navigated fairly easily. With a smartphone, you can simply download street maps, as well as MRT maps and schedules. With these simple tools you can get around conveniently, whether that means walking, taking a rideshare bike, or riding a bus or the Metro. Google and Apple Maps work quite well in Taiwan.

FLYING IN AND OUT OF TAIWAN

The airports in Taiwan are clean, well-organized, and have every service that you could want, from good dining options to clean, comfortable areas to rest and relax. The Taoyuan International Airport (TPE) *táoyuán guójì jīchǎng* (桃園國際機場) is the main airport for international travelers and is very similar to other large international airports around the world. The airport is outside Taipei in the city of Taoyuan, but it is easy to get to Taipei, or just about anywhere on the island, with numerous excellent public transportation options. The quickest and most convenient way to get into Taipei from the airport is on Taiwan's MRT. The MRT travels from the airport to Taipei Central Station in about 35 minutes. From there you can take the MRT to just about anywhere in the greater Taipei area.

Taipei Songshan Airport (TSA) *táiběi sōngshān jīchǎng* (台北松山機場) is Taipei's smaller airport, and the former international airport before the large one in Taoyuan was built. It serves other areas of Taiwan as well as some regional international locations such as cities in Mainland China, South Korea, Japan, Hong Kong, Bangkok, Kuala Lumpur, Singapore, and so on. It is conveniently located close to downtown Taipei and can be accessed via the MRT. TSA is like Reagan National Airport (DCA) in Washington, DC, or LaGuardia Airport (LGA) in New York City, and TPE is like Washington Dulles airport outside of Washington, DC, or JFK and Newark airports outside of New York City.

There are also smaller regional airports in Taichung, Kaohsiung, and Hualien. The airport in Taichung mostly serves Taiwan's outlying islands, Penghu and Kinmen, along with Hong Kong. The Kaohsiung Airport services the outlying islands as well as regional international destinations, such as Japan, South Korea, Hong Kong and Macau, cities in Mainland China, Vietnam, and so on. The Hualien Airport serves intercity travel, specifically Taipei, Taichung, and Kaohsiung.

Because of the excellent and efficient train service in Taiwan, air travel is not that practical on the main island. It is true that you can fly to Hualien from Taipei, but it is much cheaper, and actually more convenient, to take an express train. With train travel you do not have to hassle with security checks and all the waiting that's standard at airports. However, if you plan to visit any of Taiwan's outlying islands, then air travel is a good way to go. Though ferries exist to most locations, they are quite a bit slower, and if you have trouble with seasickness, then flying is a good alternative option.

OTHER TRANSPORTATION OPTIONS

When residents travel between major cities within the main island, they often utilize four main transportation methods: Taiwan High Speed Rail/ HSR (*táiwān gāotiě* 台灣高鐵), Taiwan Railway (*táiwān tiělù* 台灣鐵路), intercity bus (*guódào kèyùn* 國道客運), and driving. Those four options all have pros and cons, and residents and visitors can choose what method works better for them. High Speed Rail is very fast but costs more. Taiwan Railway costs less than High Speed Rail, but is slower. Intercity bus service is very cost effective and convenient, but it might take longer during rush hour. Many residents in Taiwan own a car, so driving is often a popular option.

> When I (Matt) am traveling in Taiwan, I generally stick to the excellent trains (high speed and regular) for traveling between cities, the fantastic MRT system in and around Taipei, taxis, and walking. I have also rented bikes and scooters in outlying areas like Hualien. Public buses are also an excellent and convenient way to get around all the major cities in Taiwan.

Taiwan High Speed Rail/HSR (táiwān gāotiě 台灣高鐵*)*

Taiwan High Speed Rail is Taiwan's bullet train system (think Japan) that runs along Taiwan's west coast, from Taipei in the north to Kaohsiung in the south, with twelve stations along the way. The railway opened in 2007, and with speeds up to 300 kmh (186 mph), previous travel times were cut considerably, as fast as 96 minutes from north to south. In Chinese it is simply known as the *gāotiě* (高鐵). The trains are clean, comfortable, and have free Wi-Fi. There are two classes: standard and business class. Most seats are reserved, but for a slight discount (about 3 percent) some cars on each train have open seating. Business-class tickets are approximately 25 percent more than standard class. Business class has larger seats, carpeted isles, padded footrests, electrical outlets, and headphone ports with streaming music options. A snack and beverage service and free reading material is also provided. Three-day passes are available on the HSR, with unlimited rides.

Since most of the HSR stations are located outside the city centers, there are usually convenient connections via shuttle buses to the regular trains, the MRT, or taxis. Tickets can be purchased at any HSR station, online (https://en.thsrc.com.tw/), as well as at convenience stores—7-Eleven, FamilyMart, HiLife, and OK Mart—28 days in advance. The online booking site is in Chinese, English, or Japanese. It is easy to navigate, and you can book tickets from abroad. When you get to the station, simply provide your confirmation information and you will be issued a boarding pass.

If you really want to have tickets in hand and bypass the HSR stations, you can try to purchase tickets via the HSR app. When you are checking out, you can choose to pay at a convenience store, either 7-Eleven or FamilyMart. You will have about 15 minutes to complete the transaction at a convenience store, using the bar code. However, when you complete your transaction at a convenience store, you won't be able to pay by credit card but will have to pay cash plus a small service fee (NT$10 per ticket, about 33 cents). When purchasing through the HSR app, you are given a bar code. After you arrive at the HSR station, you simply use your phone to scan the bar code and you are through, just like how you board flights in the United States. You can also check train schedules easily through the app. This is the preferred method of buying train tickets if you have a credit card with 3D verification.

> A word of caution: When I (Henrietta) tried to book HSR tickets online or via the HSR app, I was not able to use my credit cards because its online system requires a card with 3D verification. None of my cards (Chase Visa and American Express) has that feature. Therefore, the purchase would not go through. However, when I went to the HSR counter to purchase the tickets, the cashier would accept any of my credit cards. I hope the payment system of the HSR app no longer requires 3D verification by the time you try.

Taiwan Railway (táiwān tiělù 台灣鐵路)

Taiwan's rail network encircles the whole island. Because the interior of Taiwan is very mountainous, rail lines skirt all the way around the coast, with only a couple shorter lines penetrating the interior. Like many European countries and China, major rail stations are located primarily in downtown areas of the cities in which they pass. At these stations numerous transfer options exist, including metros, buses, and shuttles.

Trains are clean, comfortable, and convenient. They also boast a 99 percent on-time rate and are one of the most convenient and quickest ways to get around Taiwan, especially for longer distances. There are seven different classes of trains in Taiwan, ranked below in order of speed and, usually, cost.

- Tze-Chiang Limited Express (*zìqiáng hào* 自強號). The fastest and most expensive, with assigned seating, air-conditioning, and, in some cases, a dining car. Most people use this class when they want to travel to another city that is close by, such as going from Chiayi to Tainan.
- Taroko Express (*tàilǔgé hào* 太魯閣號). This is an express tilting train within the Tze-Chiang class that travels from Taipei to Hualien in about 2 hours. There are no standing tickets. All seats are reserved. This class is used mostly for tourists or those traveling the east coast.
- Puyuma Express (*pǔyōumǎ lièchē* 普悠瑪列車) is named after Taiwan's indigenous Puyuma people. This is also a tilting high-speed train in the Tze-Chiang class. It is the fastest TRA train at 150 km/h (93 mph). No standing tickets; all seats are reserved. This train travels from Taipei to Taiwan's east coast and is used by tourists and others traveling the east coast.
- Chu-Kuang Express (*jǔguāng hào* 莒光號). The second-fastest class, also with assigned seating and air-conditioning. Sometimes this class is used when you cannot book a seat on the Tze-Chiang class, or if you want to save some money.
- Fu-Hsing Semi-Express (*fùxīng hào* 復興號). The third-fastest class, also with assigned seating. It has air-conditioning but is not as comfortable as the two higher classes. This class is used when traveling between small towns and villages in rural areas. The train stops at all stations.
- Local Express (*qūjiān kuàichē* 區間快車) Short- to medium-distance commuter train that runs express (doesn't stop at every station). Trains have air-conditioning, but there is no assigned seating.
- Local Train (*qūjiān chē* 區間車). Short- to medium-distance commuter train that stops at all stations. Has air-conditioning, but there is no assigned seating.

You can buy tickets for these train classes up to 14 days in advance. Tickets can be purchased online (https://tip.railway.gov.tw/tra-tip-web/tip), at any train station, and at convenience stores (7-Eleven, FamilyMart, Hi-Life, and OK Mart). The TRA website can be accessed with multiple languages, including Chinese (both traditional and simplified characters), English, Japanese, and Korean. When booking tickets online, you can then pick up your boarding pass at the train station before you depart. Day passes can also be purchased at train stations. Taiwan Rail Passes, like a Eurail Pass, can be purchased through a travel agency and offer 3-, 5-, 7-, and 10-day passes for unlimited trips during that period. These passes are best for those traveling frequently within a short period of time.

Train stations in Taiwan are clean and orderly, and offer multiple services including shopping, dining, and areas to rest. The main station in Taipei is located within a huge underground shopping mall. You are not stuck with subpar, overly expensive dining or shopping options in Taiwan's train stations.

> On a recent trip to Taiwan, my son and I (Matt) wanted to visit Hualien for a few days. Though you can fly to Hualien, train is the most efficient, and a much cheaper way to get there. We had several options to buy train tickets. Since we were staying a short walk from the Taipei Station, we simply walked over, checked out the schedule, and bought round-trip tickets for the Puyuma Express train on the spot a day or two before we left. A friend had told me about this class of train, and it offered the quickest way to Hualien. Most people in the service industries speak at least a little English, and some speak it quite well. Even if they didn't, it is not that difficult buying train tickets as all signage, including train schedules, are in both Chinese and English.
>
> The train was clean and comfortable, and we enjoyed the nice scenery whizzing by outside. The train only made a few stops. Once we arrived in Hualien, we exited the station, and I pulled up a map on my phone to check out the route to the hotel. It was a short 10-minute walk. Once we unpacked and got settled, we went out and hailed a cab to Hualien's night market. In quieter neighborhoods like where we were staying, taxis don't come by too frequently, so we walked a couple blocks to a main road and easily hailed a cab. Finding a cab for the ride home was easy as they were abundant around the night market area.

Getting Around in Taiwan   41

VIA HIGHWAYS

Taiwan is not big, but the main island itself has ten intercity highways, called *guódào* 國道 (literally "national highway"), which is similar to the interstate highways in the United States. Odd numbers are used for north–south highways and even numbers for east–west highways in Taiwan, just like the US system. The emblem used for those national highways is a plum blossom, Taiwan's national flower, and the number is written in the middle of the emblem. There are also numerous expressways and local highways throughout the island.

The two main intercity highways are National Highway Number 1 國道一號 (*guódào yīhào*) and National Highway Number 3 國道三號 (*guódào sānhào*). These two highways run north–south and connect all the major cities on the western side of the island. Number 1 National Highway is also called Sun Yat-sen Freeway 中山高速公路 (*zhōngshān gāoshù gōnglù*). Residents on the island often just call it 中山高 (*zhōngshān gāo*) or 一高 (*yīgāo*), which is the short form for the First Highway 第一高速公路 (*dìyī gāoshù gōnglù*). Number 3 National Highway is also known as Formosa Freeway 福爾摩沙高速公路 (*fúěrmóshā gāoshù gōnglù*) or simply 二高 (*èrgāo*), which is the short form for the Second Highway.

These two major highways are not "free" ways. There are tolls throughout the entire system. However, there are no toll booths anywhere on the highways; it is all electronic, called Electronic Toll Collection (ETC). Therefore, when you rent a car in Taiwan and plan to drive on highways, you should also talk to the rental car staff about renting an ETC. The toll is based on the distance you travel. The first 20 kilometers (12 miles) are free. Then it is NT$1.2 each kilometer between 20 and 200 kilometers (12 and 124 miles). Beyond 200 kilometers (124 miles), the toll drops to NT$0.9 per kilometer. However, there are no discounts during long weekends or consecutive national holidays, in order to encourage residents to utilize public transportation and reduce the traffic on the highways. Almost every car in Taiwan is equipped with an ETC card, which links to a bank account. If it does not, you can go to the FETC (Far Eastern Electronic Toll Collection Co., Ltd.) website or via ETC app to pay for the tolls by entering the vehicle's license plate and the owner's ID.

InterCity Bus (guódào kèyùn 國道客運)

When traveling on the main island via the national highways, you can utilize convenient intercity buses (*guódào kèyùn* 國道客運), which mainly run on highways. There are many licensed intercity bus companies in Taiwan, such as Capital Bus 首都客運 (shǒudū kèyùn), Kuo-Kuang Motor Transportation Company 國光客運 (guóguāng kèyùn) and Ubus 統聯客運 (tǒnglián kèyùn). These buses travel to a wide range of cities and run frequently. In addition, intercity bus fares are cheaper compared to High Speed Rail. For example, from Taipei to Taichung, the lowest train ticket price is NT$525 (around $18) via High Speed Train (47 minutes), but it costs around NT$270 (around $9) via intercity bus. Intercity bus fares change depending on the time of day. The fare is higher during rush hour and lower during off-peak times.

In addition to the cheaper fares, another advantage of taking intercity buses is that every bus company has various drop-off and pick-up points/terminals in every city. For instance, Ubus 統聯客運 (tǒnglián kèyùn) has twenty-seven drop-off and pick-up points in Taipei City, seventeen in New Taipei City, thirty-nine in Taoyuan City, and forty in Taichung. These intercity buses offer comfortable seating and free Wi-Fi. Newer buses are also equipped with charging ports.

Driving in Taiwan

In 2022, when I (Henrietta) returned to Taiwan after almost three years of the COVID pandemic, I decided to drive from Taipei to Hsin-chu, Taichung, Chiayi, then back to Taipei. I wanted to experience what it was like to drive in Taiwan nowadays. I flew into Taipei Songshan Airport from Tokyo, Japan, and my nephew met me at the airport and lent me his car. I picked up the car and was a little bit nervous because I had not driven in Taiwan for almost three decades.

The roads going to the highways from Songshan Airport were a bit confusing, as my GPS had not adjusted to the local streets yet. But slowly and steadily, I made it to Number 1 National Highway (yīgāo 一高). Google GPS worked quite well in Taiwan after it was adjusted. However, it took me some time to get used to how Google pronounced names of streets and highways, like 國道一號 (guódào yīhào, Number 1 National Highway) or 濱江街 (bīnjiāng jiē, Binjiang Street). I was driving southbound on the highway and was quite lucky that day because I was driving against the traffic. I followed the GPS on my phone and finally made it to my first stop, Hsin-chu.

The road conditions and how people drive in Taiwan have changed significantly since the 1990s when I owned a car and was driving almost every day in Taipei. Unlike the old days, drivers in Taiwan today are polite and follow traffic rules. After driving from Taipei to Hsin-chu while I was still jet-lagged, I felt confident and at ease when I drove from Hsin-chu to Taichung.

Fantastic Highway Rest Stations

During the time I was driving on the highways in Taiwan, I was reminded how different and wonderful those rest/service areas along the highways were, compared to those in the United States. Those 休息站 (*xiūxi zhàn*, literally "rest station") or 服務區 (*fúwù qū*, "service area") are so convenient, fun, and enjoyable! You do not need to exit the highway, and you have access to gas, plenty of restrooms, and, most importantly, good food! Inside those stations, you can find gourmet coffee from a real café, bubble tea from a popular tea shop, freshly baked bread from a nice bakery, local specialties sold in different shops, and street food or hot entrées like noodle soup or pork chop rice plate from various food vendors. The options are plentiful.

The length of 國道一號 (*guódào yīhào*, Number 1 National Highway) is 374.3 kilometers (232.6 miles), and there are six rest areas 休息站 (*xiūxizhàn*). On average, you can find one every 60 kilometers (37 miles). 國道三號 (*guódào sānhào*), Number 3 National Highway has seven rest areas, spread along the 431 kilometers (268 miles) without counting the extensions. My favorite rest area is Qingshui Service Area near Taichung on National Highway Number 3.

When I stopped at Qingshui Service Area on my way to Lukang (鹿港 *lù gǎng*), I bought some fresh grapes and persimmons from a small fruit vendor outside the service building. After I went inside the building,

Qingshui Service Area near Taichung. *Image courtesy of Henrietta Yang*

I regretted so much eating a giant purple rice roll 飯糰 (fàn tuán) for breakfast that morning because I saw delicious bakery items displayed beautifully inside a bakery and was craving them. On the way back from Lukang to Hsin-chu, I stopped at Xihu Service Area, which has its own characteristics and options.

If you have a chance to drive on Taiwan highways, I highly recommend you stop at the service stations. It will be a memorable experience.

TAIWAN'S METRO SYSTEM (JIÉYÙN 捷運)

There are five metro systems in Taiwan: Taipei City, New Taipei City, Taoyuan, Kaohsiung, and Taichung, which opened its first line in April 2021. The Taipei, New Taipei, and Taoyuan lines all run together, making one huge system. The Taoyuan line runs from Taipei's central station to the airport, with various stops in between. New Taipei City's metro is an extension of Taipei City's metro system. Obviously the metro system in and around Taipei is the largest and most used. After the expansive Taipei Metro lines, Kaohsiung has the next-largest metro system, with two metro lines and a circular light rail line, with several more lines planned. Two of Kaohsiung's metro stations, Formosa Boulevard and Central Park, have been ranked in the top ten in the world for beautiful metro stations. The new Taichung Metro currently has one line with more planned for the future.

Taipei Metro (Taipei Mass Rapid Transit or MRT,
táiběi jiéyùn 台北捷運)

The MRT in Taipei is truly world-class. It is meticulously clean (no eating allowed), and people line up according to carefully marked waiting areas and actually wait until others disembark before boarding. It is astonishingly orderly, and Taiwanese people are very polite. MRT has six lines that access every corner of Taipei and beyond. You seldom have to wait more than 5 minutes for the next train, and on top of all this, it is very inexpensive. Anyone who has been to Taipei will tell you how traveling on the MRT is such a nice experience. It is similar to metro systems around the world, but provides a better experience because it is so clean, safe, orderly, and convenient.

There are basically two ways to pay your fare on Taipei's MRT. For occasional use, it is easiest to use the kiosks inside any station to buy a one-way ticket. At the kiosk you can select Chinese or English. You simply select the location where you wish to travel, and it will display the fare. Insert your money, and your change along with a plastic coin-shaped token will be dispensed. You simply run this token over a reader at the entrance to the MRT and you are admitted through the turnstile. Pocket the coin and insert it into a slot on your way out.

Using the EasyCard (*yōuyóu kǎ* 悠遊卡) is probably the most convenient way to travel in Taiwan's larger urban areas. The EasyCard is a contactless smartcard (using RFID technology) that can be used for the MRT as well as most Taiwan Railway system trains, public buses, the Ubike bike-share program, convenience stores, department stores, supermarkets, taxis, and so on. In fact, over 10,000 retailers in Taiwan accept the EasyCard. It looks like a typical debit-type card, but with fun graphics. You can buy them at any MRT station and just about any convenience store, like the ubiquitous 7-Eleven or FamilyMart, for a cost of NT$200 (NT$100 for deposit, 100 ready to be used). Once you have the card, you can easily add money (in NT$100 increments) to it at any convenience store or MRT station where there are ATM-like machines for this purpose. Simply place the card over a reader and it will display the balance. Insert money into the machine and that amount is added to your balance. Every time you use

A Taipei MRT ticket gate. *Image courtesy of Matthew B. Christensen*

A Taipei MRT platform. *Image courtesy of Matthew B. Christensen*

A Taipei MRT entrance. *Image courtesy of Matthew B. Christensen*

it, your balance is shown. When it gets low, just top it off with whatever amount you choose. To use it to ride the MRT, pass it over the sensor at the fare gates both entering and exiting. The amount deducted depends on the distance of your trip. It works the same for public buses; a reader will scan your card and show you the remaining balance. For purchases in stores, use it like a debit card—no questions asked. The vast majority of MRT and bus trips are paid for with the EasyCard. It really is convenient and efficient.

> When I (Henrietta) traveled in Taiwan in 2019, I found out that big chain stores issue their own cards that function like the EasyCard (*yōuyóu kǎ* 悠遊卡). After I purchased some snacks at *yìměi* 義美 (one of the biggest food production brands in Taiwan, with many stores throughout the island), they offered to sell me a store card (NT$50, but I would get a 10 percent discount on my entire purchases that day and in the future) that bears the logo of that store. I could even use it to ride the MRT. When the funds in the card ran low, I could go to a convenience store to add more, just like the EasyCard. So, when I was traveling with a colleague from the United States who had no MRT cards, I offered her the card I got at *yìměi* 義美 when we were taking the MRT.

PUBLIC BUSES (*GŌNGCHĒ* 公車)

City buses are clean, convenient, and air-conditioned, with comfortable seats and well-planned routes. Once you get the hang of them, they are a great way to get around. Destinations are usually displayed on an LED sign, usually in Chinese and English. The Taipei bus system actually has fifteen different systems, so not everything is standardized like the MRT. Sometimes romanized locations are different, and some buses may not always have destinations displayed in English. Bus stops are found along major and minor roads throughout the city. On Taipei City buses you either pay when you are boarding or when you disembark. There should be signage indicating which is the case. The character 上 (*shàng*) means board, and the character 下 (*xià*) means disembark. You can pay with cash (coins) or an EasyCard, and fares are determined by distance.

If you are visiting for a short time, it is best to use Google Maps or other guides to the system to determine where you want to go, rather than trying to figure out the complete system, as it is quite complex. You can get just about anywhere in the greater Taipei area with few transfers. If a bus has a colored letter or Chinese character, such as a red "R" or the Chinese character for red, 紅 (hóng), this means that the route will pass by the MRT red line at some point.

BICYCLES

Youbike (sometimes printed as Ubike, or in Chinese *wéixiào dānchē* 微笑單車, literally "smile bike") is Taipei's bikeshare program, run by the Giant Bicycles company. Pick up these orange bikes at any Youbike station and then return it to any station in the system. To register to use these bicycles, you must have an EasyCard and a local phone number. For a one-time rental, you can also use a credit card. If you do not have a local phone number but have contacts in Taipei, you can use their local number. Or if you are staying in Taipei for a short time, there are many bike rental companies that you can use as a tourist. You can register at any Youbike kiosk, which are located all over Taipei and New Taipei City, often near MRT stations and tourist sites. Once you have registered, simply select a bike, swipe your EasyCard, and slide the bike out. When finished, slide the bike into an empty terminal and wait for the LED indicator light to flash blue, then swipe your EasyCard to complete the rental. Your fare is displayed and the amount deducted from your card. Cycling is a great way to get around the city and see much more than riding underground in the MRT. Combined

A Ubike station in Taipei. *Image courtesy of Matthew B. Christensen*

with the MRT and buses, you can go anywhere quickly, conveniently, and inexpensively. Under Taipei's city planning, there are many scenic bicycle paths designed for Youbikes throughout Taipei City and New Taipei City. These paths allow you to ride all over the city without having to deal with traffic. It's a popular recreational activity for residents.

Bicycling Infrastructure in Taiwan

Some regard Taiwan as the cycling capital of Asia, and with good reason. There is excellent infrastructure for cycling in Taiwan all over the island. The most famous example of this is Taiwan's Cycling Route 1, a signed 968-kilometer (602-mile) bicycle route that circumnavigates the entire island. The route consists of dedicated bike paths, less used country roads, and larger roads with marked bicycle lanes. It was created to encourage and support recreational cycling. The entire trip typically takes between 9 and 12 days to complete. Though camping is possible along the way, you can easily get away with staying in small inns and hotels. Food and drink is never far away. An added bonus if you are considering this route is the easy availability of renting a bike. Giant, the huge bicycle company, has approximately 300 stores all over the island that rent touring bikes, complete with panniers (bags that attach to the bike to carry your gear). You can rent a bike at one shop and literally drop it off at any other Giant shop on the island. This way you can ride as far as you like.

There are a number of other bicycle paths in Taiwan that are popular with cyclists. Taipei has a network of bicycle paths that exceeds 100 kilometers (62 miles), many of them following rivers. These paths include Tamsui River Left Bank Path; Dahan River and Xindian River Bike Paths in New Taipei City; Old Caoling Circle Line Bikeway, also in New Taipei City; Dongshan River Bike Path in Yilan County; Sun Moon Lake Bike Route in Nantou County; Chishang Dapo Pond and Blue Line Bike Path in Taitung County; Dongfeng Bicycle Green Way in Taichung City; Jiji Green Tunnel and Around-Town Bikeway in Nantou County; the Dapeng Bay Bike Path in Pingtung County; and numerous other popular routes that are not necessarily bike-specific routes. There are literally hundreds of excellent bicycle routes around the island.

Cycling has become a very popular form of recreation in Taiwan. It can also be a convenient way to commute or get around the city. Though traffic can be intimidating in Taiwan, most drivers are courteous.

On a recent trip to Taiwan (2019), my son and I (Matt) visited Hualien. We wanted to explore a canyon for some river tracing and swimming. We rented bicycles at a place near the train station. We spent the day riding through the countryside, meandering our way up to Emerald Valley. We passed through farmland, small towns, and forested areas along the way. Once outside the city of Hualien, the roads and narrow lanes were quiet, with very few cars. It was ideal riding. It was also nice to see country life in Taiwan up close. After our hike and swim, we rode back to the city and to the beach. If you are somewhat fit and enjoy cycling, then a bicycle is a great way to get around. It is fast enough that you can travel pretty far, but slow enough to allow you to really take in the surroundings and interact with people.

SCOOTERS, SCOOTERS, AND MORE SCOOTERS
(*MÓTUŌCHĒ* 摩托車)

Scooters are everywhere in Taiwan. The first time I (Matt) went to Taiwan, easily one of the things that made the biggest impression on me was the number of scooters on the streets of Taipei, literally thousands of them taking up almost the entire road. During rush hour, scooters far outnumber cars and any other vehicle. There are good reasons why scooters are so popular in Taiwan.

Scooters, scooters, and more scooters. *Image courtesy of Matthew B. Christensen*

First, there is excellent infrastructure for scooter riding in Taiwan. There is ample, designated scooter parking, and the roads and intersections were designed to accommodate scooter traffic. Second, it is a cheap and convenient way to get around. A new scooter will cost you around $2,000 to $3,000, and gasoline is cheap, so getting around and commuting by scooter may even cost less than using public transportation, in the long run. Third, the developed parts of Taiwan are pretty flat and accessible, so getting around on a scooter is easy and can be done year-round because there is no snow or ice to deal with. Finally, because housing is relatively expensive in Taiwan and parking is extremely limited in big cities, owning a scooter instead of a car eases your overall expenditures, and you do not have to worry about parking like you would with a car. You will be in good company riding around the city on a scooter, as there are literally thousands of others doing the same thing.

It is also possible to rent a scooter for a day or a couple days. Most touristy places have scooter rental shops. You need an international driver's license, preferably one for motorcycle/scooter use. If you have this, it is easy to rent one for the day.

> When my son and I (Matt) visited Hualien, we wanted to explore Taroko Gorge, but we are not the types to enjoy organized group tours so we headed to the area around the train station and rented a scooter for the day. You do need to have an international driver's license to rent a scooter, but they are easy to get in the United States. A quick visit to AAA to fill out some forms, and we both had what we needed. Just be sure to get an international driver's license for scooters and motorcycles. We rode the 30 kilometers (19 miles, about 40 minutes) to the Gorge along a nice highway with wide scooter paths on the side, then rode up into the Gorge and spent the day exploring on our own. The scooter was an excellent and reasonably priced way to get around. It was certainly much cheaper than hiring a car and driver or taking the bus, which has predetermined stops. The scooter allowed us to go wherever we wanted, and we could stop for as long as we wanted.

TAXIS (JÌCHÉNG CHĒ 計程車)

Taxi services are available in most Taiwan cities. They are a quick and convenient way to get around. Taiwan's taxis, especially those in big cities, are well-known for their cleanliness and polite taxi drivers. The main taxi company in Taiwan is called Taiwan Taxi 台灣大車隊 (*táiwān dàchēduì*).

If you cannot find a taxi on the street to hail, or if you want to arrange a pick-up in advance, you can call 55688 with a cell phone or 405-88-888 with a pay phone or landline. If you are staying at a hotel, you can also have the front desk or concierge make the arrangements for you.

Another convenient way to get a taxi is by using the computer kiosks in most 7-Eleven and FamilyMart stores. Though these kiosks are only in Chinese, they are a quick and convenient way to arrange a taxi to pick you up at that 7-Eleven or FamilyMart. The kiosk will display how soon the driver will be there, usually within a few minutes. If you are having trouble, a clerk in the store can usually help out.

Rideshare companies like Uber also operate in Taiwan. With a US Uber account, you can get Uber rides in Taiwan and have the fares charged to your US credit card account.

TRAVEL TO TAIWAN'S OUTLYING ISLANDS

There are four primary outlying islands that you can visit in Taiwan. North and west of Taiwan and quite close to the Chinese Mainland province of Fujian are the Matsu Islands (馬祖 *mǎzǔ*), consisting of two main islands, Beigan (北竿 *běigān*) and Nangan (南竿 *nángān*). West of Taiwan, adjacent to the city of Chiayi are the Penghu Islands (澎湖 *pénghú*), and southeast of Taiwan are Green Island (綠島 *lǜdǎo*) and Orchid Island (蘭嶼 *lányǔ*). All of these islands are accessible by air or ferry. Flights are quick and convenient, and ferry travel offers a more laid-back approach. Some ferries do not run during winter or stormy weather.

The ferry to the Matsu Islands leaves every evening at 11 p.m. from Keelung and takes about 10 hours. Ferries to Penghu leave from the west coast, either Chiayi or Kaohsiung. The Chiayi to Magong Port (the capital of Penghu) trip takes about 90 minutes, and the ferry from Kaohsiung takes about 5 hours. Ferries to Green Island and Orchid Island leave from Kenting in the far south of Taiwan and Taitung on the southeast coast and take about an hour. Fares are reasonably priced. There are also various ferries between the Chinese Mainland and Taiwan.

> On a recent trip to Taiwan (2019), I (Henrietta) wanted to visit the Penghu Islands, which I visited once in 1992. My mother went with me. We flew out from Songshan Airport in Taipei City. The flight duration from taking off to landing was less than 1 hour. It was so easy to travel via Songshan Airport, with very minimal security checks. The

airfare was so cheap! My mother qualified for a special fare, called *jìnglǎo piào* (敬老票, literally "honor elderly citizens ticket"). Her round-trip ticket price was less than $70 (NT$2,048); mine was around $122 (NT$3,686). The flight was smooth and quick.

Even if you do not speak Chinese, it is still relatively easy to get around in Taiwan. Most forms of travel, including the trains and subways, have English signage, and if you do get lost, literally or figuratively, most Taiwanese are happy to help. In fact, you may not even have to ask for help before a polite Taiwanese person approaches you and asks if they can be of assistance.

Table 3.1. Useful Phrases

Taoyuan International Airport (TPE)	*táoyuán guójì jīchǎng* (桃園國際機場)
Taipei Songshan Airport (TSA)	*táiběi sōngshān jīchǎng* (台北松山機場)
Taiwan High Speed Rail (HSR)	*táiwān gāotiě* (台灣高鐵)
Taiwan Railway	*táiwān tiělù* (台灣鐵路)
Tze-Chiang Limited Express	*zìqiáng hào* (自強號)
Taroko Express	*tàilǔgé hào* (太魯閣號)
Puyuma Express	*pǔyōumǎ lièchē* (普悠瑪列車)
Chu-Kuang Express	*jǔguāng hào* (莒光號)
Fu-Hsing Semi-Express	*fùxīng hào* (復興號)
Local Express	*qūjiān kuàichē* (區間快車)
Mass Rapid Transit (MRT)	*jiéyùn* (捷運)
EasyCard	*yōuyóu kǎ* (悠遊卡)
Public buses	*gōngchē* (公車)
To board	*shàng* (上): *shàngchē* (上車) "to board a bus/a train/a taxi"
To disembark	*xià* (下): *xiàchē* (下車) "to disembark a bus/a train/a taxi"
Youbike aka Ubike	*wéixiào dānchē* (微笑單車, which literally means "smile bike")
Scooters	*mótuōchē* (摩托車)
Taxis	*jìchéng chē* (計程車)

4

TAIWAN'S FOOD SCENE

The Taiwanese are every bit as passionate about food and eating as any culture in the world. Social life seems to revolve around eating. If the Taiwanese are not actually eating, they are probably thinking about what they will eat next. Eating, especially eating street food, seems to be a national pastime.

The Chinese have a saying, *mín yǐ shí wéi tiān* 民以食為天, meaning "to the people, food is heaven," or "food is the most important thing in society." The Taiwanese place a great emphasis on food and eating. In fact, nearly any social or business occasion typically revolves around a meal. Taiwanese also insist on freshly prepared food, so cooking is an important skill to have if you want to eat well at home. However, because eating out is so inexpensive and usually high quality, many Taiwanese eat out much of the time, especially younger people.

When I (Matt) went to Taiwan for the first time, I had a list of thirty night-market dishes I wanted to try. I had been hearing for years from friends and colleagues about the amazing culinary scene in Taiwan. On that first visit my daughter was living in Taiwan and was constantly raving about the food. I had a colleague friend from Tainan who would tell me all about the food scene in that city. Knowing that I was a foodie and interested in Chinese culinary culture, another friend practically begged me to go to Taiwan and eat at the night markets. I had former colleagues living in Taiwan promising to take me out to eat and show me around.

I flew in from Guangzhou where I had been doing some Cantonese food research. I checked into a small business hotel a couple blocks from the famous Shilin Night Market (士林夜市, *shìlín yèshì*). After settling

寧夏夜市 (níngxià yèshì, Ningxia Night Market). *Image courtesy of Henrietta Yang*

in, I walked over to the market with my notebook and that list of thirty things I wanted to try, all pretty famous dishes in Taiwan.

Five days later I had managed to eat my way through about sixteen of the items on my list. I would hit one of the various night markets in the greater Taipei area at about 5 p.m. when they opened, sample a bunch of different dishes, walk for a bit, maybe head back to my hotel to rest up, then hit another night market at 9 or 10 p.m. for round two. It was an eye-opening experience and so different from what I was used to in Mainland China.

TAIWAN FOOD AS REGIONAL CUISINE

If there is any region of Mainland China that has influenced Taiwan cuisine the most, it would undoubtedly be Fujian cuisine. This makes perfect sense as Fujian Province is the closest part of China to Taiwan, just across the Taiwan Strait, a mere 177 kilometers (110 miles). More Taiwan residents have Fujian, or Minnan (Southern Min), roots than any other part of China. After the Nationalists lost the Chinese Civil War to the Communists, approximately 2 million Nationalist Chinese troops and refugees fled to Taiwan. They came from various parts of China and brought with them their local dialects, customs, and cuisine. For this reason, many Chinese regional cuisines, such as Sichuan, Hunan, Cantonese, and Huaiyang (Shanghai) can be found in restaurants in Taiwan. While it is possible to find good Cantonese, Sichuan, or Shanghai-style dumplings in Taiwan, it is also possible to find uniquely Taiwan and Taiwan aboriginal cuisines.

TAIWAN'S TAKE ON CHINESE FOOD

Taiwanese-style food can best be described as fusion, or Chinese food with Taiwanese characteristics. Because of Taiwan's long history of contact with the outside world, including Japan, Korea, and the West, many dishes have incorporated characteristics of those outside influences.

A good example of this is Taiwan's famous oyster omelet (蚵仔煎 kēzǎijiān). I (Matt) had recently been in the city of Chaozhou in China's far south and decided to try an oyster pancake at a typical downtown restaurant. It was okay but unremarkable, consisting of a plain egg omelet with fresh oysters mixed in. When I traveled to Taiwan and ordered one at a night market, it was a completely different dish. The Taiwan variety is made with a sticky and somewhat gelatinous pancake-like base made with tapioca starch. This batter is poured over the slightly cooked oysters then topped with eggs and leafy greens. Once it has cooked, it is drizzled with a sweet ketchup-based sauce that may include sweet chili sauce, soy sauce, maybe even a little peanut butter, and topped with cilantro. It has a soft, chewy texture (that the Taiwanese refer to as QQ), with little nuggets of fresh oysters embedded in the egg-and-pancake base and that sweet, tangy sauce. It was quite remarkable, and not what I was expecting.

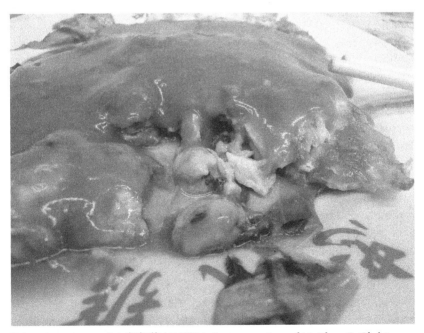

Taiwan's oyster omelet (蚵仔煎 kēzǎijiān). *Image courtesy of Matthew B. Christensen*

Another example is Taiwan's famous and delicious "tempura" (甜不辣 *tiánbúlà*). The name of this dish is actually a transliteration of the Japanese tempura, which was introduced to Taiwan during the Japanese occupation. The Taiwanese took this Japanese dish and made it their own, and today it does not really resemble tempura much at all, though it is similar to Japanese oden. It is actually fish cakes and is made by molding fish paste into various bite-size shapes, then deep-frying, boiling, or grilling it. It goes well with a sweet chili sauce. The Taiwanese love the chewy QQ texture and the sweetness of the sauce. You can find *tiánbúlà* (甜不辣) in a night market, a small eatery place, or even in a convenience store.

Eating in the Chinese world is a group-oriented, social affair. In the West we order our own dish and eat it ourselves. But in Taiwan and China, typically one person will order a number of dishes for everyone to share together. This makes for a fun, socially interactive meal.

TAINAN, TAIWAN'S TRADITIONAL SWEET TOOTH CAPITAL

Tainan, the original capital of Taiwan, is considered by many to be the cultural heart of Taiwan. Some Taiwanese also regard it as the culinary capital of Taiwan. Many of the famous night-market foods found throughout Taiwan actually come from Tainan, including coffin bread, milkfish, Taiwanese meatballs, Danzai noodles, tofu pudding, braised pork over rice, and oyster omelets, to name a few. Another Tainan specialty is *wǎnguǒ* (碗粿, pronounced *wagui* in Taiwanese). It's a liquidized rice pudding with bits of meat in it. Another is *càizòng* (菜粽), a vegetarian version of the popular glutinous rice wrapped in bamboo leaves. Instead of a meat filling, this version has peanuts and cilantro.

Tainan is also known for its sweets, and is sometimes referred to as the sweet tooth capital of Taiwan. The Tainanese believe that sugar and salt enhance the flavors of a food. Some even go so far as to say that a dish without sugar just doesn't taste right. For example, the famous braised pork over rice dish is soft and sweet when eaten in Tainan. Popular sweets include tofu pudding, shaved ice, homemade tapioca, homemade sweet potato and taro balls, milk teas, and a variety of sweet cakes, including the Portuguese-inspired, introduced by Japan, castella cake (think of a cross between a sponge cake and a cheesecake). And finally, glutinous rice sugar sticks *báitángguǒ* (白糖粿) are made with sticky glutinous starch, deep-fried, then coated with sugar—perhaps Tainan's version of a doughnut.

Taiwan's Food Scene   59

Tofu pudding (豆花 dòuhuā). Image courtesy of Henrietta Yang

TAIWAN'S FUSION CUISINE: JAPANESE, WESTERN, SOUTHEAST ASIAN

With all the foreign occupation and influences in Taiwan over the course of its history, it is no wonder that it is reflected in the food. There is a great deal of food and dishes in Taiwan that draw heavily on foreign influences, whether using ingredients not native to Taiwan, preparation styles, or interesting presentations. Taiwanese are creative and adventurous cooks and eaters. Taiwan's famous oyster omelet kēzǎijiān (蚵仔煎), mentioned above, is a good example of that.

Japanese food is abundant in Taiwan. Sushi bars can be found all over the island, and Japanese-style bento box lunches are ubiquitous. Convenience stores sell a variety of meals and snacks with an international flavor. You can get everything from a bowl of Japanese curry to a ham and cheese sandwich. You will also see potato chip flavors that don't exist in the West, such as Red Braised Beef Noodle Soup flavor, Thai Grilled Prawns, BBQ Pork, Salted Egg, Classic Ham, Swiss Cheese, Pepper Chicken, Kyushu Seaweed, Korean Spicy Pork, and so on.

A Korean food vendor on a university campus. *Image courtesy of Henrietta Yang*

Western food influences can be seen all over the island, too. This is most obvious in chain restaurants like Mos Burger and the interesting variety of Asian-inspired dishes you can find at places like McDonald's and Pizza Hut.

The availability of foreign-influenced cuisines can easily be found even on university campuses. For example, on the campus of National Chung Hsing University you can find a wide variety of cuisines, from Korean, Vietnamese, and Japanese to burgers, Subway, and all kinds of Taiwanese food items.

TAIWAN'S STREET FOOD PHENOMENON *XIǍOCHĒ* (小吃)

When people think about eating in Taiwan, they immediately think about Taiwan's night markets. There are night markets all over Taiwan that are open every night of the week. Eating is a big draw at these markets, as are shopping and games. *Xiǎochī* (小吃) is most often translated as "snacks," but it has come to mean much more than that. It most often refers to night market food items, usually in small, single portions. Most markets will have similar offerings, but some markets feature specialties you will not find elsewhere. These specialties are generally based on regional cuisines. Examples include Chiayi's famous turkey and rice, *huǒjīròu fàn* (火雞肉飯), and Tainan's coffin bread, *guāncái bǎn* (棺材板). You can find these dishes in markets up north, but residents of Tainan and Chiayi will be quick to tell you that their varieties are the original and best.

The underground food court at Shilin Night Market. *Image courtesy of Henrietta Yang*

In addition to traditional items, some vendors at night markets keep innovating what they offer to attract younger generations in order to survive tense competition. However, some innovations may not be very successful. For example, when my friend and I (Henrietta) visited Lukang Old Street (鹿港老街) in 2022, I was looking for my favorite night market treat, *zhūxiě gāo* (豬血糕 literally: pork blood rice cake): steamed rice cake on a stick, coated with a delicious sauce then a layer of peanut powder, and finished with a layer of cilantro. Instead of what it was supposed to be, the vendor combined *zhūxiě gāo* with *tiánbùlà* (甜不辣 fish cake). The sauces for these two items are completely different, so no matter which sauce the vendor used it would not be right. In this case, the cilantro was replaced with green onions and regular onions, which we thought was so wrong! The worst part was that there was no peanut powder on top. This new twist did not seem very successful, because the stall was literally empty. At least we thought it was awful.

Night markets vary in size from small one-street affairs to huge markets that cover blocks, and include not only narrow streets lined with vendors but also large indoor food courts with seating. One of the largest and most well-known night markets in Taiwan is the Shilin Night Market, *shìlín yèshì* (士林夜市), started in 1899, where the food court alone has more than 500 stalls and the surrounding streets contain many more. Another huge,

Pork blood rice cake (豬血糕 *zhūxiě gāo*). *Image courtesy of Matthew B. Christensen*

famous night market is the Keelung Miaokou Night Market, *jīlóng miàokǒu yèshì* (基隆廟口夜市), in the center of Keelung City. It is said that it has the widest variety of food of any night market in Taiwan, and is especially known for seafood.

Shilin Night Market (士林夜市 *shìlín yèshì*). *Image courtesy of Henrietta Yang*

Beef noodle soup (牛肉麵 *niúròu miàn*). *Image courtesy of Matthew B. Christensen*

Night market food is served from vendors typically running small stalls. Some are tiny, others quite large with indoor seating. Some markets even have large indoor areas with many tables and chairs, like the famous Smart Fish (林聰明沙鍋魚頭 *líncōngmíng shāguō yú tóu*) inside the Wenhua Road Night Market (文化路夜市 *wénhuàlù yèshì*) in Chiayi City. The wait to eat at the original store of Smart Fish can be more than 2 or 3 hours.

Table 4.1 is a list of things you should try at Taiwan's night markets, in no particular order. * indicates Henrietta's favorites; ** indicates Matt's favorites.

Table 4.1. Useful Phrases

台灣小吃	*táiwān xiǎochī* "Taiwan's street food"
蚵仔煎*	*kēzǎijiān* "oyster omelet"
蝦仁煎	*xiārénjiān* "shrimp omelet"
豬血糕*	*zhūxiě gāo* "pork blood rice cake"
甜不辣**	*tiánbúlà* "fish cake" (Taiwanese tempura)
碗粿*	*wǎnguǒ* (pronounced wagui in Taiwanese)
火雞肉飯	*huǒjīròu fàn* "turkey and rice"
棺材板	*guāncái bǎn* "coffin bread"
肉圓*	*ròuyuán* "Taiwanese meatball" (*bawan* in Taiwanese)
鹹酥雞*/**	*xiánsūjī* "salt and pepper fried chicken"
粽子*	*zòngzi* "sticky rice dumpling"
潤餅*	*rùnbǐng* "Taiwanese crepe that is savory and has vegetables and barbecue meat, rolled up like a burrito"
烤玉米*	*kǎo yùmǐ* "roast corn"
米粉湯	*mǐfěn tāng* "rice noodle soup"
花枝羹	*huāzhī gēng* "cuttlefish stew"
關東煮**	*guāndōngzhǔ* "Taiwanese oden"
大腸包小腸**	*dàcháng bāo xiǎocháng* "Taiwanese sausage wrap"
牛肉麵**	*niúròu miàn* "beef noodle soup"
擔仔麵	*dànzǎi miàn* "Danzai noodle soup"
生煎包	*shēngjiān bāo* "pan-fried pork buns"
臭豆腐	*chòu dòufǔ* "stinky tofu"
魚丸湯**	*yúwán tāng* "fish ball soup"
小籠包	*xiǎolóng bāo* "steamed soup dumplings"
胡椒餅**	*hújiāo bǐng* "black pepper bun"
滷肉飯**	*lǔròu fàn* "stewed pork over rice"
刈包	*guà bāo* "pork belly bun"
鐵蛋	*tiědàn* "iron egg"
麻糬	*máshǔ* "mochi"
鐵板牛排	*tiěbǎn niúpái* "cast-iron steak"

TAIWAN'S AMAZING FRUIT

Because of Taiwan's subtropical and tropical climate in the far south, a variety of fruits grow well there. In fact, for its land area, Taiwan grows twice as much fruit as California. The top producing fruit crops are mangoes, bananas, longans, lychees, pineapples, and watermelons. But what you may not realize is that because of Taiwan's great biodiversity, temperate fruits grow well here as well. Other commonly grown fruits include tangerines, oranges, lemons, grapes, peaches, starfruit, persimmons, guavas, papayas, dates, coconuts, apricots, loquats, and many others.[1] For this reason, you can find all kinds of fruit stands and stores all over Taiwan, and eating fruit is common. Fruit juice, smoothies, and bubble tea shops with fruit drinks are just about everywhere—in street markets and mall food courts, inside and outside train stations, and elsewhere.

Taiwan's shaved ice (very different from Hawaiian or American shaved ice) is legendary, with chains like Monster Ice satisfying your sweet tooth. Many of the shaved ice dishes are served with fresh fruit, mango being especially popular. In fact, when you talk to people either from Taiwan or foreigners who have lived there, they will often talk about how wonderful the fruit is there.

A fruit vendor. *Image courtesy of Matthew B. Christensen*

Mango shaved ice with taro and yam balls. *Image courtesy of Henrietta Yang*

Pineapple is locally grown and a famous crop, primarily in the south, and it is exceptionally good. In fact, one of Taiwan's favorite treats, and one that is a common gift to those visiting Taiwan, is pineapple cake (鳳梨酥 *fēnglísū*), a firm cake with a soft and chewy pineapple filling. The cakes are packaged in a small single-serving size, and sometimes come with elaborate packaging designed for gift giving. When Taiwanese eat pineapple cakes, they usually serve them with hot tea, especially traditional Taiwanese tea. The combination is just perfect.

> Until this day, the food items from Taiwan that I (Henrietta) miss the most are still the varieties of Taiwan's fruits and breakfast items. Every time I go back to visit, I wish I could bring that fruit back to the United States to share with my American friends. I really want them to see how different and how tasty the fruit is.

Taiwan's pineapples. *Image courtesy of Matthew B. Christensen*

WHAT IS FOR BREAKFAST?

Breakfast in Taiwan is not just for mornings. In fact, there are breakfast restaurants and stalls that are open 24 hours a day. Perhaps the biggest difference between breakfast in the United States and breakfast in Taiwan is the lack of sugar. There are some sweeter options in Taiwan, but most breakfast food is savory. Eating out for breakfast in Taiwan is quick, convenient, and inexpensive, and many Taiwanese regularly get breakfast on the go. You never have to go far to find a good breakfast. Table 4.2 is a list of popular Taiwanese traditional breakfast food items. * indicates Henrietta's favorites; ** indicates Matt's favorites.

In addition to those traditional Taiwanese breakfast items, Western bakery and sandwich shops are easily found. Bakeries, especially those in big cities like Taipei, provide a huge selection of pastries and bread made fresh every day. Some popular bakeries roll out their fresh-baked goods multiple times a day, and there is often a line waiting to buy.

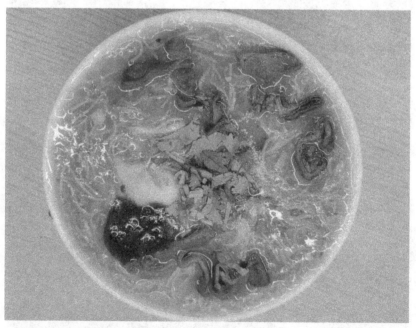

Intestine Vermicelli (大腸麵線 *dàcháng miànxiàn*). *Image courtesy of Henrietta Yang*

Table 4.2. Useful Phrases

蚵仔麵線* or 大腸麵線*	Called *mīsòa* in Taiwanese, "oyster or intestine vermicelli"
蘿蔔糕*/**	*luóbo gāo* "pan-fried radish cake with special sauce"
燒餅	*shāobǐng* "Taiwanese pita bread, typically palm-size rectangular-shaped, layered flatbread with white sesame on top"
油條	*yóutiáo* "Taiwanese churro; long, skinny fried bread sticks"
燒餅油條	A popular breakfast item: *yóutiáo* (油條) combined with *shāobǐng* (燒餅)
飯糰*/**	*fàntúan* "sticky rice ball, usually log shaped with a filling of *yóutiáo* (油條), dried turnip, and shredded dry pork"
粥	*zhōu* "congee or rice porridge, usually savory"
蛋餅*/**	*dànbǐng* "pan-fried egg rolled inside a crepe or thin pancake"
豆漿	*dòujiāng* "soy milk, a very popular drink, can be hot or cold, sweetened or unsweetened"
鹹豆漿	*xián dòujiāng* "salty soy milk"
包子	*bāozi* "steamed buns; vegetable buns or with meats, normally pork."
韭菜盒子*	*jiǔcài hézi* "chive pie; palm-size pot sticker, normally contains Chinese chive, egg, and clear noodles"
饅頭	*mántou* "steamed bun without any filling; looks like a big dinner roll. Normally Taiwanese eat it with soy milk, and very often the bun is cut open from the side and a pan-fried egg is added."
煎餃	*jiānjiǎo* "fried dumpling, usually pan-fried"
蔥抓餅**	*cōngzhuā bǐng* "scallion pancake, usually very flaky"

CONVENIENCE STORE FOOD AND FAST FOOD

On my (Matt) last trip to Taiwan, I was in Hualien on a bike heading up to one of the nearby valleys to go hiking and swimming, and my son and I decided to stop at a 7-Eleven for breakfast on the way out of town. We decided on the very popular Taiwanese oden *guāndōngzhǔ* (關東煮). This consists of fish cakes, daikon radish, boiled eggs, tofu, and sometimes other vegetables boiled in a seaweed broth. You select what you want by putting items in a small cardboard takeout container, then eat it with little skewers. I was surprised how delicious it is, and that you can find it at any 7-Eleven or FamilyMart convenience store.

On the way back into town, after riding, hiking, and swimming for several hours, it was late afternoon and we were very hungry. Rather than try to find a sit-down restaurant at the time between lunch and dinner, we stopped at a FamilyMart convenience store, picked out

Taiwanese oden (關東煮 *guāndōngzhǔ*) at a 7-Eleven. *Image courtesy of Henrietta Yang*

some freshly made meals, had them heated up for us, found a table and chairs there in the store, and had another surprisingly good meal. I had Japanese-style curry over rice. There were some schoolkids doing homework and eating snacks at the next table over.

Convenience stores and some department stores really do have a wide selection of good food that is nothing like the bad gas station or convenience store food in the United States. Some of the delicious things you can get at a 7-Eleven or FamilyMart include bento box lunches or dinners (which the staff will heat up for you), tea eggs, Taiwanese-style oden, steamed meat and vegetable buns, cold noodle dishes, onigiri (Japanese rice balls), instant ramen-type noodles with a variety of interesting flavors (hot water provided in-store), all kinds of snacks and Chinese-style bread and pastries, and finally, a huge variety of drinks, from tea to electrolyte drinks and drinkable yogurt. See chapter 5, "Living in Taiwan," for more information about convenience stores in Taiwan.

TAIWAN'S FAST-FOOD CHAINS

Taiwan's most ubiquitous fast-food brand is Bafang Yunji Dumpling *bāfāng yúnjí* (八方雲集, also known as 8way), founded in 1998 in Taipei. This dumpling and noodle restaurant has more than 1,000 locations all over the island. The restaurant serves a variety of dumplings *shuǐjiǎo* (水餃), including vegetarian pot stickers, curry-flavored chicken dumplings, Korean-style spicy dumplings, and so on. There's even a plant-based meat called Omnipork, made from rice, mushrooms, and soy and pea protein, which is very popular. Bafang Dumpling is what we would call traditional Taiwanese fast food. It's quick, convenient, and inexpensive.

Another popular fast-food chain is Mos Burger (from Japan). Mos sells hamburgers with a variety of meat (including beef patties), shrimp, fish, teriyaki, shogayaki, yakiniku, and even a chili hot dog. Some of the burgers come with a rice bun (sticky rice instead of bread). The stores also serve salads, chicken nuggets, sweet potato fries, soft drinks, and tea.

TKK Fried Chicken *dǐng guāguā* (頂呱呱) is another popular fast-food restaurant, serving fried chicken, obviously. The menu features what you would expect from a fried chicken restaurant, such as chicken sandwiches, chicken nuggets, wings, grilled and fried chicken, and family meals served in buckets.

There are a number of Western fast-food chains that are also quite popular in Taiwan, including KFC, McDonald's, Pizza Hut, and so on.

A Mos Burger store. *Image courtesy of Matthew B. Christensen*

What you might find interesting about these places, however, is the unique menu options that you won't find in the West. For example, at McDonald's you might find a ginger roast pork sandwich, honey black tea, and pineapple pie. At Pizza Hut you can find all kinds of interesting pizzas, including a seafood pizza, ramen pizza, Korean kimchi roast pork pizza, and the unique Cilantro Century Egg Pig's Blood Pizza. At KFC you might find egg tarts, sweet potato balls, and a Chizza, which is like a pizza but the crust is fried chicken and it's served with pineapple, mozzarella cheese, and chicken ham.

> When I (Henrietta) visited my first McDonald's in the United States, I went to the counter and ordered my favorites as usual: iced coffee, fried chicken, and corn soup. I still remembered the shocked look on the face of the person who took my order. He said they did not have any of the items that I ordered, but he could put filtered coffee on ice for me. I was not only surprised but also disappointed. McDonald's now has McCafé, which sells better coffee even though it still tastes different from the iced coffee in Taiwan's McDonald's. But they still do not have my favorite corn soup or fried chicken.

THE TAIWAN BOX LUNCH, *BIÀNDĀNG* (便當)

Biàndāng in Chinese means "convenient," but is also a loose transliteration of the Japanese "bento." These ubiquitous box lunches are also called bento boxes. They originated in Japan and were brought to Taiwan by the Japanese during their half-century occupation. Originally served on or around train stations, now you can find them all over Taiwan. They consist of a portable lunch with a protein or two (often a pork cutlet, a chicken drumstick, sausage, or fish), rice, some green vegetables (often cabbage), a soy-marinated egg, some pickled vegetables, and so on. Good ones are really tasty, but you can also find cheap, greasy, not very appetizing ones as well. The Taiwan Railway Administration (TRA) sells these convenient lunch boxes on trains. Train stations throughout Taiwan also have vendors selling these tasty meals. Though they are best when eaten hot, they are not bad eaten at room temperature, so are great to take on outings as well. Some areas of Taiwan are well-known for their famous bento boxes, including Chíshàng (池上) in the southeast (famous for its rice), Fènqǐhú (奮起湖) on Ali Mountain outside Chiayi (famous for its local produce), and Fúlóng (福隆), northeast of Taipei in New Taipei City (famous for its braised pork belly). Incidentally, all three of these places are on train lines. But you don't

A Chiayi turkey rice bento box. *Image courtesy of Henrietta Yang*

necessarily have to travel to these areas to sample these delicious lunch boxes. The Chíshàng (池上) boxes can be found all over the island now. Taiwan box lunches are definitely worth a try; many Taiwanese love them and eat them on a regular basis.

EATING HOT POT, *HUǑGUŌ* (火鍋)

Eating hot pot is very popular in Taiwan, and it is a fun way to spend time with friends or colleagues. Like eating out at other Chinese restaurants, it is a group experience. With hot pot, diners actually cook their own food at their table. At a hot pot restaurant, each table is equipped with an electric pot in the center of the table for the whole group. Often the pot has a divider and is separated into two sides. One side usually has a mild broth and the other side a spicy one. Or one side can be a vegetarian soup base and the other side non-vegetarian. The pot is sometimes called a *yuan-yang* pot (*yuānyang guō* 鴛鴦鍋). At a hot pot restaurant, you select the soup base and raw ingredients (including meat and vegetables), and you basically cook it yourself in the hot pot at your table. Dipping sauces are also of your own making.

Some restaurants have a set broth that they specialize in, and others will allow you to select your broth. These may include chicken- or pork-based stock, vegetable broth, herbed pickled cabbage, Sichuan pepper (which is numbing and spicy *málà* 麻辣), and white pepper. Because of the Japanese and Korean influences in Taiwan, you can also get kombu, sukiyaki, miso, or kimchi broths. Once you have decided on a broth or broths, you will then select your ingredients. This is done by either ordering off a menu or walking over to a refrigerated room or a bank of refrigerated cases and simply selecting what you want by placing items on a tray or plate. There is also a condiments bar where each person concocts their own dipping sauce. Typical ingredients at the condiments bar include soy sauce, Japanese soy sauce (a bit sweeter), black vinegar, white vinegar, barbecue sauce (*shacha*), chopped scallions, minced ginger, chopped garlic, sesame oil, chopped chilis, chili oil, sesame paste, sesame seeds, grated daikon, and so on. Many Taiwanese like to add a beaten raw egg to their sauce.

HOW татO EAT GROUP HOT POT

Hot pot restaurants vary from high end to low budget. If specific utensils such as serving chopsticks, ladles, and tongs are supplied, use those to slide the ingredients into the bubbling broth, and again to fish out the meat and vegetables. Other places are more intimate and casual, and you simply use your own chopsticks to fish out whatever you want to eat. It is a group affair and everyone does the cooking. Whoever is hosting your meal may pick out items from the broth and place them in your bowl. Some restaurants are all-you-can-eat and others you order once. If your broth gets a little low, simply notify your server and they will add more broth to your pot. The Taiwanese have a strong love affair with hot pot. Traditionally, it was only eaten in the colder winter months, but nowadays, people eat and enjoy it throughout the year.

Another kind of popular hot pot is individual hot pot. Each diner orders and eats their own unique hot pot. It can come prepared, meaning every ingredient is already placed in the pot and is cooking in the soup base you ordered. Normally, this kind of hot pot does not require a dipping sauce because the broth already has a strong flavor. The other kind of individual hot pot is similar to the group hot pot but just a personal-size

An individual hot pot. *Image courtesy of Henrietta Yang*

one. You can still select your own soup base and meat choice, which will accompany a set of vegetables, and you will have to create your own dipping sauce like the group hot pot.

In short, hot pot is very popular in Taiwan, and since Taiwanese are extremely creative when it comes to food, there are many different kinds of hot pot restaurants on the island.

VEGETARIAN CUISINE IN TAIWAN

Taiwan is one of the most vegetarian- and vegan-friendly countries in Asia. This is due in part to the long Buddhist tradition. Many of the Taiwanese younger generation have chosen this lifestyle for health and environmental reasons. In fact, after India, Taiwan probably has the highest percentage of vegetarians (12–16 percent).[2] It is not hard to find good vegetarian or vegan food in Taiwan, and much of it is excellent. In Mainland China most of the good vegetarian food is found at or near Buddhist monasteries. In Taiwan it can be found all over the island. To tell people you are a vegetarian, you can say *wǒ chīsù* (我吃素, literally "I eat vegetables"). There are three kinds of vegetarianism in Taiwan: ovo-lacto vegetarian *dànnǎi sù* (蛋奶素),

those who do not eat meat but eat dairy products; vegan *quán sù* (全素); and semi-vegetarian *bàn sù* (半素) or *fāngbiàn sù* (方便素), sometimes called flexitarian (someone who is mostly vegetarian, but eats meat occasionally).

Especially popular are vegetarian buffets. Low-cost vegetarian cafeterias are located throughout Taiwan. You can also find high-end vegetarian restaurants. It is estimated that there are more than 6,000 vegetarian restaurants in Taiwan. Many of the popular cafeteria-type vegetarian restaurants are self-serve and you pay by weight. Rice and soup may cost extra.

TAIWAN'S TEA CULTURE

Tea trees (actually more like bushes) grow naturally in Taiwan, and Taiwan's extensive tea culture comes from its early immigrants from Fujian Province. Taiwan produces some truly world-class tea. Tea shops, where you can buy tea leaves, and tea houses, where you can sample Taiwan's famous teas, are abundant. There is a wide variety of teas found in the Chinese-speaking world, but they can basically be broken down into a few general categories based on the amount of fermentation.

Green teas *lǜ chá* (綠茶) are not fermented but are allowed to oxidize. They have a fresh aroma and are green or light green in appearance. Popular green teas include Dragon Well tea *lóngjǐng chá* (龍井茶), Biluochun tea *bìluóchūn* (碧螺春), and jasmine tea *mòlìhuā chá* (茉莉花茶). Green teas are popular in Taiwan and are most commonly drunk in Mainland China and Japan. When you are automatically served tea in Japan, it will almost always be a green tea.

Black teas *hóng chá* (紅茶), called "red tea" in Chinese, are fully fermented, have a dark red appearance, and are sweeter and may have a roasted flavor. The most common black or red tea in the Chinese world is pu'er tea *pǔěr chá* (普洱茶).

Oolong tea *wūlóng chá* (烏龍茶) is a semi-fermented tea and falls somewhere between green and black teas. It is a bit stronger than green teas and has a yellow or brown appearance. The amount of oxidation (and thus flavor) ranges from 10 percent (lighter, closer to a green tea) to 80 percent (darker, more robust, and closer to a black tea). Tie Guanyin tea *tiě guānyīn chá* (鐵觀音茶) is a common oolong tea.

Oolong tea is the most common tea drunk in Taiwan.[3] In fact, Taiwan is famous for its oolong tea. The climate and topography make Taiwan an ideal place for tea growing, especially oolong tea. High mountain tea is Taiwan's specialty, where the higher altitudes, humidity, and misty mountains produce a truly unique taste. Twenty percent of all oolong teas worldwide are produced in Taiwan. Taiwan's most famous and sought after oolong tea is Alishan High Mountain Tea *alǐshān gāoshān chá* (阿里山高山茶). It is about 40 percent oxidized and has a light brown appearance. The tea leaves are usually bunched into dense little balls that unfold when added to hot water.

Other famous and popular teas in Taiwan include Oriental Beauty *dōngfāng měirén chá* (東方美人茶), which is 60 percent oxidized and has an amber color and earthy honey flavor. When the tea leaves are harvested, small bugs called tea green leafhoppers are left on the leaves. Their bites initiate an early fermentation process that gives the tea its honey flavor. The dried tea leaves have white tips, so it is sometimes called "white-tipped oolong tea." Baozhong (Pouchong) or "wrapped variety" tea *bāozhǒng chá* (包種茶) is another favorite in Taiwan. It is 15 to 25 percent oxidized and has a light floral and melon flavor. It comes wrapped in square packages.

In addition to the traditional Chinese teas mentioned above, another kind of tea that you can find almost everywhere in Taiwan is called pearl milk tea *zhēnzhū nǎichá* (珍珠奶茶), or bubble tea or boba tea, which is very popular among the younger generations. This tea-based drink originated in Taiwan in the early 1980s, and is normally accompanied by chewy tapioca balls (aka boba or pearl) and milk. You have to drink it with a much bigger/wider straw in order to suck up the pearls. In the old days, the options of pearl milk tea were limited because the base, milk tea, was pre-mixed. Due to its popularity and people's creativity, the options on the menu of a typical tea shop today can be overwhelming. The base can be green tea, black tea, oolong tea, or fruit-flavored tea. It can be made with or without milk. There are also about a dozen different toppings that you can choose to add into your pearl milk tea. Nowadays, many pearl tea shops customize drinks based on your preference of ice level, sugar level, and topping

Pearl milk tea. *Image courtesy of Henrietta Yang*

choices such as boba, lychee jelly, coffee jelly, grass jelly, or red beans. This is a must-try when you are in Taiwan. Note that when Taiwanese or Chinese drink traditional teas, they do not add sugar or milk in their tea.

HOW TO EAT WELL IN TAIWAN

It is not hard to eat well in Taiwan, but it does take a little knowledge to know where to get the best food. As a general rule, if you want to eat authentic Taiwanese-style Chinese food, we suggest you venture out of your hotel (if you are staying in one). There are a few key things to keep in mind when searching out good food in Taiwan. How and where you eat in Taiwan will also depend a bit on whether you are an "eat to live" or "live to eat" kind of person. For the former, you can eat just about anywhere and be okay. But for those who really love to eat and want to experience the unique cuisine of Taiwan, it will take a bit more effort.

Besides the information provided above concerning night markets, convenience stores, and so on, below are some additional tips on how to find good food in Taiwan.

1. *Ask locals where they like to eat.* Wherever you are in Taiwan, there will be locals around who are passionate about eating and will gladly recommend their favorite places to eat.
2. *Go where the crowds are.* A busy restaurant is usually a reliable sign of good food. It may not be convenient to wait in a long line to eat, but you will be rewarded with much better food than the place down the street that is empty. There is a reason why good restaurants are busy.
3. *Do some online sleuthing.* There are quite a few resources online about eating in Taiwan, and many of them are in English. This includes YouTube channels, blogs, websites with eating guides to Taiwan, and so forth. A simple online search can yield useful results.
4. *Follow this simple technique.* Walk out of your hotel or apartment and turn left. Walk to the next intersection and turn left again. Start looking for a place, either restaurant or stall, where there are lots of people. The goal here is to get off the main road and into an area where locals are likely to be eating. As suggested above, pick a place that is crowded with Taiwanese people. Avoid eating at big hotel chain buffets, unless they cater to Chinese travelers.

EATING IN A CHINESE RESTAURANT

Chinese dining is a group experience. Unlike in the West, in Taiwan, one person (usually the host) generally orders a number of dishes for everyone to share. If you are out with a group of friends, you may discuss together what you would like, but one person still typically does the ordering. A Lazy Susan, *zhuǎnpán* (轉盤), is usually found in the center of the table for a big group to facilitate access to all the dishes in the center of the table. If you are out eating hot pot, then the actual hot pot will be in the center of the table.

Chinese dishes are usually brought to the table as they are prepared. A serving spoon may be provided for each dish. Diners serve themselves small portions, either onto a small plate, bowl, or bowl of rice. Plates are typically not used at restaurants unless it is more of a fast-food place, where the food may be piled onto rice on a plate. North Americans are typically used to eating Chinese food with rice, but this is not always the case in Taiwan, especially at nicer, more expensive restaurants. Diners may not have a bowl of rice during dinner; the reason is that you do not want to fill up on cheap rice when you have all these delicious dishes to eat. At restaurants like this, rice, noodles, or dumplings may be served at the end of the meal, to top you off if you are still hungry.

HOW TO MAKE SENSE OF A CHINESE MENU, *CÀIDĀN* (菜單)

Chinese menus can be challenging to decipher because Chinese dishes often have creative names that may not have anything to do with what is in the dish. For example, *yúxiāng ròusī* (魚香肉絲) "fish flavored pork" does not have any fish in it. The term *yúxiāng* (魚香), meaning "fish fragrant," is featured in a variety of dishes with spices and ingredients that are often used when preparing fish. The dish *máyǐ shàngshù* (螞蟻上樹) "ants climbing a tree or log" is another good example. You might think this dish really had ants in it, but it is actually thin rice noodles fried with bits of minced pork. The tiny bits of meat resemble ants and the noodles represent the tree or log. Even if you have solid Chinese language skills, making sense of menus can still be challenging. However, if you understand how Chinese menus are arranged, and have some basic knowledge of Chinese food, you will have more success ordering.[4]

There are three clues to look for when ordering Chinese food from a menu, based on how a dish is prepared. The name of a Chinese dish may be based on the following: (1) the central ingredient in the dish, (2) how the dish is prepared (such as steamed, stir-fried, etc.), and (3) how the ingredients are cut or sliced.

A typical menu at a nicer Chinese restaurant may be arranged in the categories shown in table 4.3, with the character 類 (*lèi*) meaning "category" or "type."

Table 4.3. Useful Phrases

類	*lèi* "meaning category or type"
特色菜	*tèsè cài* "special dishes"
冷菜/冷盤	*lěng cài/lěng pán* "cold dishes (often appetizers)"
海鮮類	*hǎixiān lèi* "seafood dishes"
肉類	*ròu lèi* "meat dishes"
雞鴨類	*jī yā lèi* "chicken and duck dishes"
豬肉類	*zhūròu lèi* "pork dishes"
牛肉類	*niúròu lèi* "beef dishes"
羊肉類	*yángròu lèi* "lamb dishes (particularly at Muslim restaurants)"
素菜	*sù cài* "vegetable dishes or vegetarian dishes"
豆腐類	*dòufǔ lèi* "tofu dishes"
鐵板類	*tiěbǎn lèi* "dishes cooked on an iron platter"
飯麵類	*fàn miàn lèi* "rice and noodle dishes"
主食類	*zhǔshí lèi* "staple food"
湯類	*tāng lèi* "soup and stew dishes"
飲料	*yǐnliào* "beverages"

How a Dish Is Prepared

Knowing how a dish is prepared can also be helpful in making sense of a Chinese menu. Not all Chinese food is stir-fried *chǎo* (炒) in a wok. The cooking methods listed in table 4.4 are commonly used, and sometimes appear on a menu.

Table 4.4. Useful Phrases

炒	chǎo "stir-fried"
清炒	qīngchǎo "fresh stir-fried, usually with no sauce"
清炒菠菜	qīngchǎo bōcài "fresh stir-fried spinach"
家常小炒	jiācháng xiǎochǎo "family-style stir-fried dishes"
紅燒	hóngshāo "red-braised, stewed in a dark soy sauce blend"
紅燒排骨	hóngshāo páigǔ "red-braised ribs"
糖醋	tángcù "sweet and sour"
糖醋排骨	tángcù páigǔ "sweet and sour ribs"
糖醋裡脊	tángcù lǐji "sweet and sour pork," lǐji meaning "tenderloin"
烤	kǎo "roast"
北京烤鴨	běijīng kǎoyā "Beijing roast duck"
蒸/清蒸	zhēng/qīngzhēng "steamed/simply steamed"
清蒸魚	qīngzhēng yú "steamed fish"
煮	zhǔ "boiled"
水煮蛋	shuǐ zhǔ dàn "boiled egg"
煎	jiān "fried in oil"
煎豆腐	jiān dòufu "fried tofu"
炸	zhà "deep-fried"
炸雞	zhà jī "fried chicken"

How the Ingredients Are Cut

Knowing how the ingredients are cut (see table 4.5) can also offer a clue to the dishes on a menu. These methods mostly refer to meat, but can also refer to vegetables. In other words, usually the vegetables are cut similarly to the meat. So if a dish has thin slices of meat, the vegetables will also usually be cut into thin slices.

Table 4.5. Useful Phrases

丁	dīng "cubed or diced"
宮爆肉丁	gōngbào ròudīng "Kung Pao pork"
片	piàn "sliced"
羊肉馬鈴薯片	yángròu mǎlíngshǔ piàn "lamb with sliced potatoes"
絲	sī "shreds," literally means "silk"
韭菜炒肉絲	jiǔcài chǎo ròusī "chives stir-fried with shredded pork"
塊	kuài "meat cut into pieces, usually with the bone"
炸雞塊	zhà jī kuài "fried chicken"
排	pái, literally means "row" or "line" and usually refers to ribs
烤羊排	kǎo yáng pái "roast lamb chop"

Not all dishes will offer these clues. If you speak some Chinese, you may want to ask your server what the special dishes *zhāopái cài* (招牌菜) are, meaning the dishes that the restaurant specializes in. These are also referred to as *náshǒu cài* (拿手菜). Many restaurants are known for certain dishes. If you do not speak any Chinese, another strategy is to nonchalantly observe what others around you are eating, then point to those dishes. Finally, in many restaurants it is common to have picture menus with both Chinese and English. This can apply to nice sit-down restaurants as well as small hole-in-the-wall places where the pictures may be on the wall. In these cases, simply point and you are good to go.

Chinese dining can be quite different from dining in the West. Whether you are eating in a restaurant, at a banquet, or at someone's home, the following rules of etiquette should be followed for a smooth dining experience.[5]

- Chinese dining is usually a group experience. Dishes are normally served family style with a Lazy Susan in the center of the table (tables are usually round). This provides easy access to all the dishes. Do not reach across the table; wait for the dish to make its way around to you. Eat from those dishes close to you, then when the Lazy Susan is rotated, select from those dishes within easy reach. Refrain from taking too much of any one dish.
- Make sure your chopsticks are free of grains of rice or other food bits before reaching to take more food. If serving spoons or chopsticks are provided, use those to serve your food from the plates in the center of the table.
- It's common to bring your rice bowl up to your mouth when eating, pushing the rice into your mouth with your chopsticks. Trying to pick up rice with your chopsticks and bringing it up to your mouth usually makes a mess with rice falling all over the table.
- Do not stick your chopsticks into your rice perpendicular to the table, as this resembles incense sticks used for worship at temples.
- If meat is served with the bone, place bones (and shells) in a neat pile near your plate or rice bowl. Some restaurants will supply a small plate for this. At home, sometimes a small bowl or container is on the table, so cleanup is simple.
- Fish is usually served whole with the head and tail intact. Once one side of the fish has been consumed, someone will carefully turn it over.

- It's not polite to take the last thing on a plate. Someone will usually offer the last bit to someone. Diners will usually politely decline, suggesting the person offering take it. If the offers persist, it's okay to reluctantly take the last bit off a plate.
- It is polite to eat whatever is served you, even if you do not like it. You do not have to eat a lot of it, but at least give it a try. Declining an offer is considered rude and may offend your host.
- Soup in a large communal bowl is typically served by dipping the serving spoon into the pot from the back; that is, dip the spoon into the pot from the back edge of the spoon to the front. When eating soup, it is polite to sip the soup from the spoon, but do not put the whole spoon in your mouth.
- Tea is almost always served at a Chinese meal, particularly dinner. Other beverages may or may not be served. Chinese generally believe that drinking at a meal is not good for your digestion, especially ice water.
- Toothpicks are often provided at the end of a meal. Cover your mouth with a hand when picking food from your teeth.
- Banquets and large meals at restaurants conclude with fresh fruit. This is your sign that the meal is over. Other than fresh fruit, eating dessert after a meal is not common.
- It is considered a privilege to pay the bill when eating out at a restaurant with friends. At the conclusion of a meal, a friendly argument often erupts over who will pay the bill. Once the meal is finished, you usually need to ask for the bill by saying *mǎidān* (買單), *jiézhàng* (結帳), *suànzhàng* (算帳), or simply *duōshǎo qián* (多少錢) "how much?" Usually several in the party will insist on paying the bill. Sometimes the argument can get fairly animated, with one person trying to give their card to the server only to have another person push it away and offer their card. In the end, one person will pay the bill. If you are with a group of friends, even if you paid the previous time, it is still appropriate for you to offer to pay the bill, but everyone is aware that you paid last time and will not expect you to pay again. It is becoming more common for friends to each pay for their own meal, but this is usually at more informal places where each person has their own plate of food.

Table 4.6. Useful Phrases

民以食為天	*mín yǐ shí wéi tiān* "Food is the God of the people."
夜市	*yèshì* "night market"
士林夜市	*shìlín yèshì* "Shilin Night Market"
基隆廟口夜市	*jīlóng miàokǒu yèshì* "Keelung Miaokou Night Market"
綠茶	*lǜ chá* "green tea"
龍井茶	*lóngjǐng chá* "Dragon Well tea"
碧螺春	*bìluóchūn* "Biluochun tea"
茉莉花茶	*mòlìhuā chá* "jasmine tea"
紅茶	*hóng chá* "black tea, called 'red tea' in Chinese"
普洱茶	*pǔěr chá* "pu'er tea"
烏龍茶	*wūlóng chá* "oolong tea"
鐵/烏龍茶	*tiě guānyīn chá* "Tie Guanyin tea"
阿里山高山茶	*ālǐshān gāoshān chá* "Alishan High Mountain Tea"
東方美人茶	*dōngfāng měirén chá* "Oriental Beauty"
包種茶	*bāozhǒng chá* "Pouchong or 'wrapped variety' tea"
珍珠奶茶	*zhēnzhū nǎichá* "pearl milk tea or bubble tea or boba tea"
便當	*biàndāng* "box lunch"
火鍋	*huǒguō* "hot pot"
鴛鴦鍋	*yuānyāngguō* "a pot with a divider in the middle"
麻辣	*málà* "numb and spicy"
我吃素	*wǒ chīsù* "I am a vegetarian."
蛋奶素	*dànnǎi sù* "ovo-lacto vegetarian"
全素	*quán sù* "vegan"
半素	*bàn sù* "semi-vegetarian"
方便素	*fāngbiàn sù* "flexitarian"
Lazy Susan	*zhuǎnpán* (轉盤)
menu	*càidān* (菜單)
special dishes	*zhāopái cài* (招牌菜) or *náshǒu cài* (拿手菜)
ask for the bill	*mǎidān* (買單), *jiézhàng* (結帳), *suànzhàng* (算帳), or simply *duōshǎo qián* (多少錢) "how much?"

5

LIVING IN TAIWAN

This chapter provides readers with a general overview of the types of housing in Taiwan and offers insight into the important etiquette you need to know when you are invited to a Taiwanese home. In addition, it covers how to safely and effectively look for a place to stay and what to expect when you study or work in Taiwan. We also provide practical information that will help you take care of your daily needs easily and efficiently.

HOUSING OVERVIEW

As of May 2023, Taiwan's population was 23,361,084. Seventy percent of the population live in the following six special municipalities (*zhíxiá shì* 直轄市), which are directly under the control of Taiwan's central government: New Taipei (*xīn běishì* 新北市, population 4,021,983), Taichung (*táizhōng* 台中, population 2,831,323), Kaohsiung (*gāoxióng* 高雄, population 2,735,456), Taipei (*táiběi* 台北, population 2,501,988), Taoyuan (*táoyuán* 桃園, population 2,299,339), and Tainan (*táinán* 台南, population 1,858,092).[1] Like most residents in big cities such as New York City, residents in these six special municipalities in Taiwan mostly live in high-rise apartment towers or traditional apartment buildings. Living, renting, or buying a stand-alone single-family home or a two- or three-story townhouse in big cities in Taiwan is impossible even for rich residents because land is scarce and extremely expensive. As a Chinese saying goes: *cùntǔ cùnjīn* (寸土寸金, literally "inch land inch gold," meaning land is as expensive as gold). Therefore, American-style single-family houses are just not available in big cities. However, the farther away from city centers, especially outside those six special municipalities, the easier and more likely it

A neighborhood in Taipei. *Image courtesy of Matthew B. Christensen*

is to find stand-alone single-family houses or townhouses. When you go to study or work in Taiwan, it is most likely that you will live in an apartment.

The general layout of an apartment home for Taiwanese families ranges from small two-bedroom/one-bathroom units in traditional apartment complexes to more spacious four-bedroom/two-bathroom homes in newer apartment towers. Of course, they all have kitchen and living room spaces; however, size varies. Within an apartment, the room that Westerners might find hardest to adapt to is the bathroom. Commonly, bathrooms are not equipped with a bathtub or an independent shower stall due to limited space. In Taiwan these are called wet bathrooms. A shower head, a sink, and a toilet are all part of the same space, and everything tends to get wet when you shower. The downside of this kind of bathroom is that floors stay wet for some time after showers. In newer or high-end apartments, a hotel-style bathroom is available, which means there is a divider between the shower space and the sink and toilet, so the floor is not constantly wet. Because of these traditional-style bathrooms, many Taiwanese have designated slippers or plastic slides for bathroom use only. Taiwanese, like Japanese, are very obsessed with indoor slippers. Take my sister's home, for example:

> My (Henrietta) sister lives in a high-rise apartment tower with three bedrooms, two bathrooms, one living room, one kitchen, a space for a

dining table, and a balcony next to the kitchen with the washing machine. (Taiwanese usually do not use dryers. They hang their laundry on the balcony.) When I go to her home, I have to remove my shoes outside before stepping into the living room, then I put on a pair of indoor slippers. To use the bathroom, I first remove the indoor slippers for the living room area outside the bathroom and change to the bathroom slippers (actually more like plastic slides). Of course, I have to change back to the living room slippers before I return to the living room area. I would be scolded if I stepped out of the bathroom with the bathroom slippers on. If I am going to the balcony, I have to change to the "balcony slippers," which are "outdoor" slippers because the balcony area is an open space. My sister has actually loosened up her slipper policy in recent years. I remember when she first moved into that apartment twenty years ago; she even had specific slippers for the kitchen because cooking oil or sauce might drop onto the floor when cooking, and that might stick to the slippers. Therefore, those slippers could not be used in the living room.

For Westerners, wearing shoes inside their homes is a common practice. However, that is not what the majority of Taiwanese do at home. Please note that it is very rude to step inside a Taiwanese home with outdoor shoes on when the homeowners remove their shoes and change into indoor slippers. Therefore, be prepared to remove your shoes when you visit Taiwanese homes. In addition, change to bathroom slippers if they are present in the bathroom.

Another thing to be aware of is the kitchen. Many landlords who rent apartments to tenants, especially students, only provide an electric hot plate in the kitchen to discourage indoor cooking. But this should not be a big issue since eating out in cities is so convenient and inexpensive, and not many students are interested in serious cooking anyway.

ON-CAMPUS VS. OFF-CAMPUS

When you go to Taiwan to study or work for a longer period of time, if it is not already arranged by the university or company, one important task is finding a place to stay. If the university or company offers dormitory options, it would be a good idea to take it for the first month or so, in order to settle in more quickly. After you get to know the environment better, you can move out if you do not like the accommodations. Unlike universities in China where you can find building after building of dormitories for international students on campuses, universities in Taiwan generally do not have designated dormitory buildings for international students. If they do, the space is quite limited or mainly for degree-seeking students or official exchange students. If you are just there for a short-term language study, say one semester, the chances are you will have to look for an apartment yourself, or there might be certain housing space off-campus where the university's language program may have an agreement.

It is possible to look for an apartment even if you have never been to Taiwan. First, you can ask colleagues in Taiwan for recommendations if you are going there to work, or you can ask local language program coordinators to provide you accommodation information if you are joining a Chinese language program. Nowadays, language programs may offer useful information on their websites. For example, the Chinese Language Division in the Language Center of National Taiwan University has a web page about accommodations and insurance.[2] On this page, you can find a document in both English and Chinese about what you need to be aware of when renting a place. It also includes tips on how to select a safe place and what to know when signing a lease. In addition, it provides recommended websites for options for short-term stays and room/apartment rentals for a longer stay.

Many foreign students find their stays through websites that they are familiar with, such as Airbnb.[3] A colleague of ours from the San Francisco area found a nice Airbnb apartment in the Beitou area in Taipei, which is well-known for hot springs, for his one-semester sabbatical leave. He was very happy with that accommodation and said he actually had a hot spring in his apartment!

Taiwanese people often use the following sites when hunting for an apartment:

- 591租屋網 *zūwū wǎng*: https://rent.591.com.tw/?kind=0&region=1
- 崔媽媽租屋網 *cuī māma zūwū wǎng*: https://rent.tmm.org.tw
- 好房網 *hǎofáng wǎng*: https://rent.housefun.com.tw

After you get to Taiwan, you will quickly realize how widely Facebook is incorporated into Taiwan people's daily lives. People who are looking for housing might join several Facebook groups to look for roommates or to sublease or lease directly from landlords. Information posted on Facebook changes every day and there are more units available than on some websites. Below are some Facebook groups focusing on the Taipei area:

- 大台北租屋網房東盡量 po: https://www.facebook.com/groups/305665579858865/
- 一起住吧！大台北合租分租租屋交流社團: https://www.facebook.com/groups/1834309463450416/
- 台北租屋、出租專屬社團: https://www.facebook.com/groups/464870710346711/
- 台北合租屋: https://www.facebook.com/groups/481382605221218/
- 大台北好好好租屋網: https://www.facebook.com/groups/359576301158357

The only issue with Facebook groups and the websites listed above is that the information is mainly in Chinese. Of course, this is a good opportunity to practice your Chinese; however, it might also cause some misunderstanding or miscommunication if you are not familiar with the terminology related to rental properties or leasing contracts. You may need to enlist the help of a Chinese-speaking friend or colleague.

HOTELS

Many well-known international chain hotels are present in Taiwan, such as Marriott, Hilton, Hyatt, and Sheraton, which tend to be located in convenient locations in big cities. In addition to these big chains, Taiwan also has a wide variety of hotel choices, from Taiwan's own chain hotels to small boutique hotels and luxury resorts to hostels on the other end of the spectrum. Because of Taiwan's convenient transportation system, you do not necessarily have to stay right next to where you are visiting (university or business).

In recent years, when I (Henrietta) go back to Taiwan, I like to explore different kinds of hotels in different parts of the cities I visit. For example, I stayed at the Caesar Park Hotel, a chain hotel in Taiwan, near Banqiao train station, a couple times for its convenient location. I wanted to avoid staying near the Taipei train station because of the busy crowds. Caesar Park Hotel was literally less than 5 minutes' walk to both the High Speed Rail Station (which I needed when I traveled to Chiayi to visit our partner university) and the MRT (which I needed when going to Taipei to visit other universities).

In 2019, I tried a very unique hotel near Taipei City Hall. Its name was WXYz (Woolloomooloo Xin Yi snooZe). The hotel has only six

A hotel room in WXYz. *Image courtesy of Henrietta Yang*

Tea in a pitcher for a bath soak at Teascape. *Image courtesy of Henrietta Yang*

or seven rooms on the second floor. Its first floor is divided into two parts: one side is a tiny grocery store featuring Western products such as cheeses and salami; the other side is a cafe selling Western-style breakfast, lunch, and dinner. On the third floor is an exhibition hall. During my stay, there was an exhibition of photos and art works about light and colors. I visited the exhibition, which was free, and really enjoyed it. I had a Japanese-style room, and there was a compact sitting area right outside my room, where kitchen and laundry facilities were available. My stay at this hotel was memorable and enjoyable.

Another unique and interesting hotel I stayed at in recent years was called Teascape in Chiayi. It is a Taiwan chain hotel that integrates lots of local culture and art into its interior design. The theme of the hotel I stayed at in Chiayi was "tea" (hence Teascape). Chiayi is at the base of A-Li Mountain, which is well-known for its high mountain tea. Inside the hotel room, you could bathe in tea!

I (Matt) tend to avoid the big chain hotels and enjoy staying in smaller boutique or business hotels. I usually select them based on location and unique features. The rooms can be small, but they have always been clean, neat, and comfortable. I often use Hotels.com to book my rooms in Taiwan.

In addition to a hotel's own website, we often use the following sites when booking rooms in Taiwan:

- https://www.hotels.com
- https://www.agoda.com
- https://www.eztravel.com.tw

LONG-TERM RESIDENCE IN TAIWAN

If you will be in Taiwan for an extended period, in addition to a visa (either a student visa or work visa), you will also need an Alien Residence Certificate (ARC). This card serves as your identity card as a foreigner living legally in Taiwan. This is something you apply for after arriving in Taiwan. The process is relatively straightforward. You simply go down to the nearest city or county police headquarters closest to where you are living with the appropriate documents (which include your passport, visa, proof of residence, and possibly other documents), fill out the forms, and in about two weeks your card will be mailed to you. This must be done within 15 days of your arrival. Having this card will allow you to open a bank account, and will make it easier to buy tickets, use rideshare bikes, rent scooters, and so on.

TAKING CARE OF DAILY NEEDS

Living in Taiwan, especially in big cities, is fun, convenient, and safe. By doing a little homework you can find a district and neighborhood that will suit your needs, whether you are a student or working. Once you have settled into an apartment, dorm, or hotel, it will be a fun experience to get acquainted with the neighborhood. Each neighborhood has just about everything you could need: convenience stores, coffee and tea shops, cafés and restaurants, nearby transportation options, parks, and so on. You do not need a car to get around in big cities. Various modes of transportation are widely available throughout the cities. (For more information about transportation in Taiwan, see chapter 3.)

Most cities in Taiwan are densely populated. Unless a building is designated as business use only, oftentimes residential and business uses are mixed, especially those buildings along major streets or roads. It is common to have the first floors of a building (called *diànmiàn* 店面, literally "shop face") used as offices, clinics, restaurants, salons, or shops, and the rest of the floors as residential apartment units. Even in small alleys between buildings, you can find small cafés for breakfast, coffee shops, bakeries, or convenience stores. It is very convenient to live in cities because shops and stores near your apartment are generally sufficient for your daily needs. Two neighborhood businesses deserve your special attention—post offices and convenience stores—because they are very different from what you are familiar with in North America.

Post Offices

Post offices in Taiwan have many unique functions and services that post offices in the United States do not have. In addition to providing all kinds of postal services, post offices in Taiwan go further by providing banking and life insurance services. Many Taiwanese like to open saving accounts with post offices because of good interest rates and convenient locations. Unlike big banks, post offices are often tucked away in residential areas, where you can deposit money, wire payments, and exchange currency. Post offices in Taiwan also sell life insurance!

Convenience Stores

Another business that can be found everywhere in Taiwan is the convenience store (*biànlì shāngdiàn* 便利商店) such as the 7-Eleven (Taiwanese affectionately call it *xiǎoqī* (小七) "little seven" in Chinese or "Seven" in English), FamilyMart (*quánjiā* 全家), and Hi-Life (*lái'ěrfù* 萊爾富). They are very different from those in the United States and are usually open 24 hours every day.

In general, there are about six convenience stores for every square kilometer in Taipei City. The red, orange, and green "7-ELEVEN" sign can easily be found all over Taiwan, even in rural areas. If you go to live in Taiwan, you will fall in love with convenience stores, especially 7-Eleven and FamilyMart. Each store is usually small and compact (the minimum required store space is about 132 square meters (1,423 square feet), but the services it provides and the items it carries are beyond many foreigners' imaginations. Therefore, when you are looking for housing, if there is a convenience store nearby, it is an extra bonus because you will benefit greatly from its extensive services.

A typical Hi-Life store in Taiwan. *Image courtesy of Henrietta Yang*

Coffee Shops

In addition to tea, Taiwanese people also drink a lot of coffee. Before the first Starbucks landed in Taipei City in 1998, most coffee shops were heavily influenced by Japanese coffee shops and were for affluent people in the city and for special occasions. In the last two decades, Taiwan has experienced a coffee shop boom. All kinds of coffee shops have emerged, from chain stores to unique boutique coffee shops, and the new Taiwanese coffee culture has embraced not only Japanese trends but also Western styles like American Starbucks and European boutique cafés. The density of coffee shops in Taipei is definitely comparable with that of convenience stores.

Banking and Money

There are a couple different ways to manage your money while in Taiwan. When you first arrive and until you get your Resident Alien Card (described earlier), you can simply use any ATM to withdraw local currency from your bank at home. There are ATM machines everywhere, including at banks, convenience stores, train and MTR stations, and many other places. Once you have your Resident Alien Card you can open a bank account. You will need that card, your passport, and proof of residence. When you open an account, you will be given an ATM/debit card and a passbook. Make sure you get an ATM card with the Visa debit card function. The passbook (a small passport-like book that records all your transactions) is nearly obsolete these days. Some older people still use them, but with online banking they are not used much, if at all.

If you are working, most employers require you to have a bank account so your salary can be directly deposited. Opening an account can be a little stressful, especially if you don't speak Chinese and the teller does not have good English. If that is the case, it's a good idea to bring a Taiwanese friend, classmate, or colleague with you to help out.

Phones and Sim Cards

There are a couple ways of dealing with phone communication in Taiwan. If you are there for a short visit, it is probably easiest to just have an international plan, though that can get expensive if you are using it for longer periods of time. If your phone is unlocked, it is easy to use your own phone and buy a SIM card in Taiwan. They are relatively inexpensive and can be bought at any cell phone store (which are found everywhere). Another option is to buy a Taiwanese cell phone. They are very good and have all the features you may want. Likewise, they are relatively inexpensive. If you go this route, you can just plan to use that phone for the duration of your stay in Taiwan.

Trash and Recycling Collection

Trash collection in Taiwan is like nowhere else in the world. When you hear "Für Elise," grab your trash bags and head to the street. Taiwan has a policy of "trash is not allowed to touch the ground." Residents are required to buy blue plastic bags (very inexpensive) to dispose of their trash. There are no trash cans and no traditional collection practices. Instead, fleets of bright yellow trash collection trucks, followed by smaller white recycling trucks, travel through neighborhoods 5 days a week. You will hear one of two tunes, the familiar Beethoven's "Für Elise" or "Maiden's Prayer" by the Polish composer Tekla Bądarzewska-Baranowska. When you hear the music, you bring your carefully sorted trash and recycling outside where a group of your neighbors will have assembled. The workers place various bins on the side of the street for such things as paper, plastic, metal, raw food (for composting), and cooked food scraps (for pig feed). Many residents use this opportunity to catch up with their neighbors, gossip, and just socialize. Most public trash cans were eliminated to encourage people to be more careful about how much trash they create and what they throw out. This system also forces residents to be vigilant about recycling. In fact, Taiwan has the second-highest recycling rate in the world (after Germany).

Public Toilets

Both Chinese and Western-style toilets are used in Taiwan, and many public restrooms offer a choice. Paper towels and toilet paper are not always provided. You should always carry your own supply. The signs for restrooms are as follows: Toilets, W.C., 洗手間 (*xǐshǒu jiān*, literally "wash hands room"), 廁所 (*cèsuǒ*), 男 (*nán* "male"), 女 (*nǚ* "female").

The 7-Eleven Phenomenon in Taiwan

> I (Henrietta) still remember how excited I was when I saw the first red, orange, and green 7-Eleven sign in Southern California (because that was my favorite store in Taiwan!) and how disappointed (and shocked) I was after I saw what was inside the store. I naively assumed 7-Eleven

stores in the United States would be similar to those in Taiwan, so I went in with lots of joy but came out with so much disappointment! In my heart, I was yelling, "Something is wrong! This is not 7-Eleven! It's not cute at all, and there's no delicious food!" I think I gave another 7-Eleven a try to see if the first one was just a mistake. After visiting the second one in the United States, I haven't been to a third one since then.

People in Taiwan love 7-Eleven convenience stores. It was the first 24-hour convenience store chain in Taiwan and now has the most stores on the island. At the time of writing, there are about 6,210 7-Eleven stores alone on the island![4] Competition among convenience stores is fierce. Some stores even try to stand out by creating their own unique decor in order to attract customers and survive in the highly competitive market.

When 7-Eleven stores were first introduced in 1978, they were like other convenience stores, mainly focusing on selling snacks, fast food, drinks, some personal hygiene products, and daily necessity goods. Over the past couple decades, the food items sold at 7-Eleven have evolved and now carry significant Japanese cultural influences. When Westerners think about food from a convenience store, it is mostly food items like hot dogs, potato chips, or sugar-coated pastries. But food sold at 7-Eleven in Taiwan covers a wide selection: from microwave food items to sushi in the refrigerated section to delicious oden *guāndōngzhǔ* (關東煮) in a boiling pot. Oden

A 7-Eleven near National Taiwan University. *Image courtesy of Henrietta Yang*

Some food options at 7-Eleven. *Image courtesy of Henrietta Yang*

is traditionally Japanese and consists of fish balls, fish cakes, deep-fried tofu, hard-boiled eggs, radish, and so on, in a soy-based dashi broth. These food items, including the microwave food items, are surprisingly tasty.

Nowadays, 7-Eleven has its own "food hall" *xiǎoqī shítáng* (小七食堂) in the store. Customers can find traditional Taiwanese lunch boxes *biàndang* (便當), such as Taiwanese-style pork chop bento and stir-fried seafood noodles, or international cuisine like Thai chicken bento and Korean fried chicken stir-fried rice, all at very reasonable prices, between NT$55 and NT$85 ($2–$3).

In addition to food, 7-Eleven has its own in-house coffee and tea shop called City Café. Even people in rural areas can purchase good-quality coffee from 7-Eleven's City Café, which has a variety of espresso coffee drinks. In addition to coffee drinks, 7-Eleven's City Café also offers freshly brewed tea in order to compete with the widespread tea shops, which sell the so-called *shǒuyáo chá* (手搖茶), literally "hand shake tea."

When I (Henrietta) went back to Taiwan to visit my sister several years ago, one morning she told me that she was going to a convenience store downstairs to get coffee and wanted to know if I wanted some. I thought she was going to get that kind of canned coffee, which was very popular in Taiwan. So I told her no. When she returned, I saw a cup of beautiful and delicious latte! I was so surprised and had to ask her again if that was from the convenience store downstairs. She said yes. Apparently, espresso drinks were already available everywhere in convenience stores at very reasonable prices!

To get most chores done in Taiwan, you only need to go to "little seven," which is truly more than a convenience store. In fact, it has developed into a service platform, both in-store and online, to help residents on the island take care of many daily household errands. It has become a one-stop shop and, most importantly, is conveniently located in neighborhoods or outside metro stations. Some interesting services include the following:

Shipping service. In Taiwan, to send a package, whether domestically (via Black Cat delivery) or internationally (via DHL or FedEx), you do not have to go to a post office or FedEx store. 7-Eleven can take care of that conveniently. The shipping service even includes returning online orders and receiving online orders as well.

Payments. 7-Eleven can process all kinds of payments, including traffic tickets, tolls, auto tag fees, parking tickets, phone bills, and water bills! Additionally, it even assists financial institutions, insurance companies, and charities to collect payments or donations. 7-Eleven goes the extra mile to provide payment services to foreign laborers from the Philippines, Vietnam, Thailand, and Indonesia.

Ticket center. 7-Eleven sells all kinds of tickets, including concert tickets, train tickets, movie tickets, and workshop admission fees, for a very small fee. Popular online game cards can also be purchased here.

Copy, fax, and photo service. Customers can upload documents or images through a mobile app, online platform, or a kiosk (ibon) in-store and pick up printouts there. They can even easily create customized postcards via ibon! 7-Eleven also provides fax services, both sending and receiving.

Laundry. Some 7-Eleven locations even offer laundry service where you drop off your dirty clothes, then go back later to pick them up.

It is unbelievable how many things a tiny 7-Eleven can do, so it is not difficult to imagine that 7-Eleven has its own app and online platform where many more services and products can be found, such as mobile phone service, hotel booking, and its own product lines (UNIDESIGN). In today's highly competitive convenience store market in Taiwan, stores try very hard to go beyond just selling products and services in order to survive. Now, more and more 7-Eleven stores have added public toilets and seating in their stores for customers to sit down, rest, and have a cup of coffee or tea.

I (Henrietta) had been very curious about what other services or food items "little seven" could come out with. When I went back to visit in 2019, I went to a 7-Eleven in a residential area near National Taiwan University where my students were staying. To my surprise, there was a book corner where the top ten bestselling books were on display. Customers could also buy books there. Next to the book section, there was a bakery section! I could literally spend an entire afternoon in that 7-Eleven reading one of the bestselling books while having a cup of latte and a slice of delicious cake.

A book corner inside a 7-Eleven. *Image courtesy of Matthew B. Christensen*

In order to survive in a fiercely competitive market, many of the services offered at 7-Eleven are also available at FamilyMart and other convenience stores as well.

Before I (Matt) went to Taiwan for the first time, I had heard all about 7-Eleven and FamilyMart convenience stores. I was not disappointed. Even being the foodie that I am, I found the food at 7-Eleven and FamilyMart to be pretty good. I would often head to the local 7-Eleven to grab a quick delicious breakfast of oden or some decent bread. One day, after cycling around the Hualien countryside, it was between lunch and dinner, so I headed to a local FamilyMart and had a tasty bowl of Japanese curry. I was surprised that you could find real food at a convenience store.

HEALTH AND SAFETY

Taiwan's National Health Insurance (NHI) is one of the best, with low costs, high participation rate (99 percent of the population), and excellent, efficient, and timely care. Participation in the program is mandatory, with high approval ratings. A big advantage of this health insurance is its low cost, which is partially based on level of income. Those workers with low incomes are 100 percent subsidized, so they pay nothing. Co-pays are low, and maximum out-of-pocket expenses are also capped at reasonably low rates. Another benefit is that NHI covers nearly everything, from preventive care to specialized treatment. Some residents may secure additional private insurance to cover some highly specialized treatments not covered under NHI. Western as well as traditional Chinese medicine is covered by the insurance. Even though most health-care providers in Taiwan are private, almost all work with the NHI, so you can go to just about any doctor you wish, be it a general-care practitioner or a specialist. Another big benefit to the program is that you seldom have to wait long to get an appointment. In many cases you can schedule an appointment with a doctor or clinic and be seen the next day. In order to have services provided, you must present your NHI card at the time of your visit.

For a foreigner to be eligible for NHI, they need to have resided in Taiwan for six consecutive months. You are allowed to leave the country for a maximum of 30 days, but the total time of residence must equal or exceed 180 days before applying for benefits. Once you qualify, you receive the same benefits as any other Taiwan resident.

Traditional Chinese Medicine

Traditional Chinese medicine (TCM) is a mainstay within the health-care system in Taiwan. Traditional Chinese medicine takes a holistic approach to healing and has been around for thousands of years. Rather than treating the symptoms, TCM attempts to address the cause of the symptoms and focuses on wellness and balance throughout the entire body. A traditional Chinese doctor will examine a patient and seek to determine the cause of the illness and how it relates to other functions in the body. The emphasis is on balance in the body and is based on the principles of *yin* and *yang*. For example, too much *yin* (or cold) in the body causes an imbalance. The five elements (air, earth, fire, metal, and wood) are also integral to TCM and are part of the life force, or *qi*, that flows within our bodies. The *qi* of the elements waxes and wanes in the body in daily and seasonal cycles.

For example, if you have a stomachache, the problem may not necessarily be in your stomach. TCM strives to figure out what is causing the stomach pain, and may treat some other area of the body, which will then reduce the stomach pain. Western medicine tends to focus on symptoms and may treat the stomach pain, causing it to go away temporarily, but it may not solve the problem or the cause of the pain.

TCM consists of two main branches or forms of treatment: Chinese herbal medicine and external methods such as massage, cupping, acupuncture, qigong, and so on. Taiwan has many traditional Chinese herb shops or pharmacies. Based on your ailment, the pharmacist will create a blend of herbs that are usually steeped in hot water and drank like tea. These remedies can be very effective, though some may also be based on superstition.

Acupuncture is commonly practiced in Taiwan, China, and wherever Chinese people live. It is an effective and proven method to relieve all kinds of injuries and ailments, including pain relief, repetitive injuries like carpal tunnel syndrome, skin problems, autoimmune disorders like Crohn's disease, respiratory problems like asthma, as well as many other issues.

In recent years cupping therapy has gained widespread popularity, especially among elite athletes. It is effective in reducing pain, improving blood flow, and relaxing the muscles. I (Matt) have used cupping therapy for many years. It is especially effective for loosening up stiff neck and shoulder muscles after hours on a cramped plane. I also find it effective at reducing stress. Massage is a very popular form of therapy as well, and massage clinics can be found all over Taiwan. They even have small massage shops near night markets where you can get a quick neck and shoulder massage.

In Taiwan, the NHI covers both Western and traditional Chinese treatments, and many hospitals provide services for both.

Tips to Stay Healthy

Your time in Taiwan will be infinitely more enjoyable if you remain healthy. The following tips (developed after working with literally thousands of students) will help you stay healthy while in Taiwan.

- Stay hydrated. Taiwan is very hot and humid in the summer months. Make sure to stay hydrated by drinking plenty and perhaps carrying around a refillable water bottle or thermos. It is not recommended that you drink tap water. Use bottled water, a filter, or boil all tap water.
- Be aware that some common prescription medications like Adderall are illegal in Taiwan. There are also rules on how much prescription medication can be brought into the country. If you are taking prescription medications, do a little research and find out what and how much you are allowed to bring into the country.
- The Centers for Disease Control and Prevention website has useful travel information for Taiwan. Be sure to get the recommended immunizations.[5]
- Adjust to the new time zone as quickly as possible.
- Be careful what you eat. Taiwan is a safe and clean place, but there can be places where things are not as sanitary. Busy places typically have fresher food.
- Be social. Get out. Make friends. Be active.

NATIONAL HOLIDAYS

Taiwan has many official holidays to celebrate traditional festivals or to commemorate historic events. Traditional festivals are based on the lunar calendar, so they fall on different days of the Western calendar every year. On the other hand, historic events, like the 228 Incident, are based on the Western calendar. Here are the major holidays that are observed by Taiwan's government, starting from January:

- January 1: New Year

Living in Taiwan 103

- Chinese New Year (春節 *chūnjié*), based on the lunar calendar (it usually falls somewhere between mid-January and mid-February)
- February 28: To commemorate the 228 Incident
- April 4: Children's Day
- April 5: Tomb Sweeping Day (清明節 *qīngmíngjié*)
- May 5 (lunar calendar): Dragon Boat Festival (端午節 *duānwǔjié*)
- August 15 (lunar calendar): Mid-Autumn Festival or Moon Festival (中秋節 *zhōngqiūjié*)
- October 10: Taiwan's National Birthday

Among those holidays, the most important one is Chinese New Year. Normally, this is a weeklong holiday, starting from New Year's Eve. For tourists, it is recommended to avoid visiting Taiwan on New Year's Eve and the next 3 days because this is the most important family holiday for Taiwanese. Shops and restaurants will be closed, and residents are spending time with their families. It is like Thanksgiving Day or Christmas Day in the United States, but longer.

Even though Thanksgiving and Christmas are not official holidays in Taiwan, Taiwanese embrace those holidays as much as Americans, especially the younger generations. Restaurants roll out all kinds of Thanksgiving and Christmas special feasts, and department stores have elaborate decorations and promotions to attract customers.

A store selling traditional Chinese lanterns. *Image courtesy of Matthew B. Christensen*

USEFUL APPS AND SOCIAL MEDIA

- Line: Taiwanese use Line to call, text, video chat, and share pictures and documents. It is free to download and to use. The major difference between Line and WhatsApp is that Line has tons of cute "stickers" that users can add to express their emotions, kind of like emojis, but much cuter.
- Facebook: In Taiwan, almost all business utilizes Facebook. I (Henrietta) personally do not use Facebook, and it was inconvenient when I visited some stores in Taiwan because the first thing the store staff asked for was my Facebook account. They wanted me to log into my account so I could see their store information.
- Useful apps for transportation: YouBike, Uber, T-EX 行動購票 (for High Speed Rail), 台鐵 e 訂通 (for regular trains), and EasyCard (for MRT).

Table 5.1. Useful Phrases

New Taipei	xīn běishì (新北市)
Taichung	táizhōng (台中)
Kaohsiung	gāoxióng (高雄)
Taipei	táiběi (台北)
Taoyuan	táoyuán (桃園)
Tainan	táinán (台南)
Convenience stores	biànlì shāngdiàn (便利商店)
7-Eleven or Seven	xiǎoqī (小七)
FamilyMart	quánjiā (全家)
Hi-Life	lái'ěrfù (萊爾富)
Restrooms or toilets	xǐshǒu jiān (洗手間, literally "wash hands room"), cèsuǒ (廁所)
Male	nán (男)
Female	nǚ (女)
Lunch boxes	biàndāng (便當)

6

STUDYING IN TAIWAN

Before you go to Taiwan to study or to work, it is important to gain a basic understanding of the role of education in Taiwan's society and families. This knowledge will help you comprehend the education system and certain phenomena you will encounter on a campus or at a workplace in Taiwan.

THE VALUE OF EDUCATION IN TAIWANESE SOCIETY

Traditional Chinese society values and respects people who achieve academic success, and scholars and intellectuals are commonly rewarded with high social status. This traditional value on Chinese education was brought to Taiwan by ethnic Chinese from Mainland China 400 years ago and has deeply influenced how Taiwanese view education. Education credentials are still considered one of the most critical elements that define a person's intellectual capability in Taiwan, especially when they do not yet have any work experience. Therefore, children are repeatedly reminded in their early years that they must study hard and pursue higher education if they want to be successful in the future. Needless to say, academic learning is the most essential matter for children in Taiwan during their upbringing.

> Like most Taiwanese children at that time (1970s and 1980s), especially those in big cities, my (Henrietta) only duty during my upbringing in Taiwan was to study diligently. Nothing was more important than academic learning. Playing sports or instruments was not important because they did not play a role in high school or college entrance examinations. Therefore, I completely missed my "critical period" for learning many

skills that most American children would consider "basic skills," such as riding a bicycle or swimming. I still do not know how to ride a bicycle. Thanks to my roommate at graduate school in the United States, I did eventually learn how to swim.

Because Taiwanese value education so highly, being an educator, no matter at what level, is often well respected by parents and students. Children are taught to respect their teachers *lǎoshī* (老師) beginning with kindergarten. The title *lǎoshī* (老師) is used to refer to instructors not only in K–12 but also in universities. The term *jiàoshòu* (教授) is a more formal term used for addressing professors at the university level.

Taiwanese parents, like most parents in East Asian countries, place a strong emphasis on their children's education, and it is almost always the single most important matter for parents, who will do nearly anything they can to support their children's education. When children are going through their academic journey, oftentimes what parents expect from them is to solely focus on studying and not much else. Parents generally do not involve children in household chores, nor do they expect children at senior high to go out and find part-time jobs to contribute financially, because children normally spend long hours studying, even after normal school hours. As long as it is related to education, parents do everything they can to support children financially.

> When I (Henrietta) lived in Taipei City in the 1980s and 1990s, Western franchises like McDonald's, KFC, and Pizza Hut mushroomed in the city. The target customers of these restaurants were middle-class families and white-collar professionals, and working at those fast-food chains became a cool part-time job among college students at that time. Like other college students, I was also interested in working there. However, my father refused to let me do that. To him, the money I would make would not make much financial contribution to the family, and the work experience I would gain was not significant because it was not academically related. However, when I got a part-time job as an ESL teacher at an English learning center for children, my father approved because I would be a teacher *lǎoshī* (老師).
>
> Later, when I decided to come to the United States to pursue further study, my father still thought it was his responsibility to support me financially. My sister, two years older than me, also voluntarily jumped in to support me as well. My family was just an ordinary Taiwanese middle-class family, and my example was in no way a special case. Most Taiwanese and Chinese parents would do exactly what my father did to support their children in pursuing as much education as they can.

Getting a student loan was unheard of at that time. However, now in Taiwan, due to Western cultural influences, getting a student loan is not as novel as in the past. But it still is not as popular or as common as in the United States.

In the twenty-first century in Taiwan, many from the younger generations have recognized the importance of involving their children in extracurricular activities, such as playing musical instruments and learning English, at the early stages of children's academic learning. However, the rigorous academic competition of getting into prestigious high schools and universities has not changed much. Because children are expected to earn a college degree and are encouraged to pursue advanced study overseas if they can, extracurricular activities only add additional burdens on children's already packed daily schedules. For instance, many children in big cities begin learning English and musical instruments at the preschool level.

After children start elementary school, they usually have to go to after-school learning centers every weekday, sometimes even on the weekends. These learning centers can be *ānqīnbān* (安親班) or *bǔxíbān* (補習班, literally "supplementary learning class"). The former functions as an after-school day-care center, providing tutoring on students' homework and all academic subjects covered at schools. The latter focuses on specific subjects. On the weekends, there might be more practice sessions for children to attend. Academic pressure starts as early as kindergarten in big cities. In a statistics report released by Taiwan's Ministry of Education (MOE), there were about 5,024 *bǔxíbān* (補習班) in Taiwan in the year 2000.[1] In a separate report from MOE, in 2022 Taiwan had 17,364 *bǔxíbān* (補習班) and 783 *ānqīnbān* (安親班).[2] The increase of those after-class learning centers was driven by two serious societal issues that most students and families in Taiwan face: rigorous academic competition and parents' long working hours.

Rigorous academic training is at every stage of a Taiwan student's life. Once students move on to junior high and senior high, they still go to *bǔxíbān* (補習班) after school to drill or learn more math, English, and/or science in order to pass the entrance examinations of high schools or universities.

Bǔxíbān (補習班) are very popular in Taiwan. The areas in front of the Taipei train station are packed with all kinds of *bǔxíbān* (補習班). Even after students are already at college or have begun working, many still go to *bǔxíbān* (補習班) to prepare for TOEFL and/or GRE exams if they plan to study abroad after graduation or to study the examinations for public service jobs, which are considered *tiěfànwǎn* (鐵飯碗), "an iron rice bowl." Unlike a normal rice bowl, which is made of china or clay and can break easily, a *tiěfànwǎn* (鐵飯碗) is made of metal and will never break, which implies a secure job. In Taiwan, a public service job comes with good benefits and stability, which appeals to many people, and requires job applicants to pass a government general entrance examination. A friend of mine took one year off after she graduated from college and joined one of the popular *bǔxíbān* (補習班) near the Taipei train station just to prepare for the general entrance examinations.

Another fact about Taiwanese students and their families that American students might find interesting is their housing arrangements at colleges. Unlike many students in the United States, if their schools are within a reasonable commute from their parents' homes, Taiwanese students do not move out after they start college. They do not move out and rent an apartment near the schools they attend just because they have become college students. In America, it is common for children to move out of their parents' home after high school even if the institutions they attend are located nearby their parents' houses. For instance, several of my students were from Oxford, Mississippi, a tiny college town, where the University of Mississippi is located. Normally, it takes only 10 minutes to go from one end of the town to the other. However, my students from Oxford did not live with their parents after they graduated from high school. Instead, they moved out and rented an apartment or a house with their friends in town. To me, that is not economical at all, because I am sure that my students' parents still keep rooms in their houses for their children. Nevertheless, that living arrangement is typical for college students in the United States. In Taiwan, children move out of their parents' house only when their jobs or schools are located in a city that makes a daily commute not sensible. Many Taiwanese children live with their parents until they get married. If space in the house allows, male children might even live with their parents after they get married.

On-campus housing is limited, especially in big cities such as Taipei. This is partially because it is not a common practice for college students to move out of their parents' houses, and also because public transportation makes it very convenient for students to commute. The limited on-campus housing is reserved for those from other cities or degree-seeking students from other countries. Therefore, most Taiwanese college students commute to campus, often by bicycle or public transportation. It is common to see lots of bikes on college campuses, where parking for cars is usually reserved for faculty.

A scene at National Taiwan University. *Image courtesy of Matthew B. Christensen*

Bicycles on a university campus. *Image courtesy of Matthew B. Christensen*

TRADITIONAL ASIAN PARADIGMS ABOUT EDUCATION

Chinese and Taiwanese attitudes, assumptions, and paradigms toward teaching and learning differ from the West. They are deep-seated and go all the way back to traditional Confucian values established thousands of years ago. For most of China's history, only the elite class, comprising a very small percentage of the population, had access to education. This education consisted of studying, learning, and memorizing the Confucian Classics (a series of nine books considered to be of utmost importance in society and the epitome of education).

As early as the Han dynasty (206 BCE–220 CE), this education system was closely tied to a civil service examination program. These exams were dependent on knowledge of the Confucian Classic texts, and passing these rigorous exams allowed one to enter government service and enjoy a comfortable life. This examination system was in place until the early twentieth century. It required rote memorization of the texts and regurgitating the information in lengthy and difficult exams. Those who passed at the highest levels were ensured a comfortable, even luxurious lifestyle of civil service. As such, those with an education were highly respected in society.

The modern education systems in East Asian countries (primarily China, Japan, South Korea, and Taiwan) still retain influences of the traditional Confucian educational model. As mentioned above, Taiwanese place a high value on education. Today, though, many professors in Taiwan's universities have been educated in the West. As such, their teaching methods more closely align with Western practices, and their approaches affect how students respond in class. However, there are older faculty who still adhere to more traditional Asian paradigms, which include the following:

- Heavy emphasis on tests: Oftentimes your grade depends on test scores.
- Focus on textbooks and memorization: regurgitation of material from the text to tests.
- Teacher-centered classes: This is the "sage on the stage" format where the teacher lectures and students sit quietly taking notes. There is minimal classroom interaction between faculty and students.
- Focus more on structure and facts, less on application.

During my early years of being an international student in the United States, I (Henrietta) really had a hard time participating in classroom discussions or asking questions in class because of the kind of learning environment I was accustomed to in Taiwan. I still remember how much courage I needed to build up to raise my hand to ask a question in class. My heart would be racing, and my English would be even more broken—all because I was not used to speaking in class in Taiwan.

For students of Chinese, you may find Chinese-language classes in Taiwan may vary from what you are used to in Western university curriculums. Many Chinese language programs may have the following characteristics:

- Focus on the written language: Reading and writing characters take center stage, with speaking and listening skills not emphasized as much.
- Reliance on tests for grades: with this comes greater focus on memorization.
- Focus on structure: Vocabulary and grammar are highlighted, with less emphasis on practical application.

The good news is that there are more and more young Taiwanese instructors who have visited or studied at North American institutions and have adopted a more interactive teaching method.

A class on a university campus. *Image courtesy of Matthew B. Christensen*

TAIWAN'S UNIVERSITY SYSTEM

Earning at least a bachelor's degree is expected for the younger generations in Taiwan. If you plan to study in Taiwan, you have numerous choices because the number of institutions of higher learning on the island is astonishing, especially considering the size of Taiwan. According to the Foundation for International Cooperation in Higher Education of Taiwan, in 2023 more than 1.1 million students pursued a higher education, and there were 148 universities and colleges on the island.[3] The state of California, about eleven times bigger than Taiwan, has only around 400 colleges and universities.

The number of institutions of higher learning soared from 58 in 1994 to 153 in 2016.[4] The cause for the fast expansion was due to a societal issue of overemphasizing credentials or degrees. After martial law was lifted in 1987, people in Taiwan demanded more opportunities to earn postsecondary degrees in order to get better jobs. At that time, the competition for getting into a university or college was very intense, and higher education was designed for elite students, not for the general population. More colleges and universities were needed to accommodate high school graduates. To solve the problem, residents on the island appealed to politicians who needed votes during election years.[5] With the aim of pleasing voters, politicians pushed for more and more colleges and universities throughout the island, sometimes sacrificing quality of education for quantity. As a result, the number of institutions increased almost threefold in twenty years, and the acceptance rate for colleges and universities reached almost 100 percent. From 2013 to 2022, college admission rates were above 90 percent, except for the year 2019 (81.29 percent). The acceptance rate for the year 2022 was 98.94 percent, which was a record high.[6] This kind of growth and acceptance rate created another societal issue: an excess supply in Taiwan's higher education.

Many of the universities and colleges in Taiwan are clustered in big cities, such as Taipei City (26), New Taipei City (22), Taichung City (17), and Kaohsiung City (18).[7] Master's degree programs as well as doctoral programs are common in comprehensive universities; medical schools are available in four of the comprehensive universities, such as National Taiwan University and National Cheng Kung University. There are also medical-based universities in Taiwan such as Taipei Medical University and National Yang Ming University, which merged with National Chiao Tung University in 2021, and became National Yang Ming–Chiao Tung University.

Taiwan's post-secondary system is very similar to the system in the United States. Currently, Taiwan has 68 four-year comprehensive colleges and universities (*dàxué* 大學) and 80 technological institutes (*kējì dàxué* 科技大學). Among the 148 institutions, 32 are national universities (*guólì dàxué* 國立大學) and 15 are national technological institutions (*guólì kējì dàxué* 國立科技大學).[8]

In Taiwan, most of the prestigious colleges and universities that students in Taiwan fight so hard to get into are all national public institutions. Therefore, many Taiwanese students associate "public" and "national" as better institutions than private ones. With that kind of mindset, I applied to only state universities when I came to the United States to study many years ago because state universities were somewhat the equivalent of national public universities in Taiwan. At that time, the concept of "private liberal arts colleges" was not a familiar term to many Taiwanese. However, I believe more and more people in Taiwan are aware of those now.

A typical four-year comprehensive university in Taiwan, like one in the United States, consists of various colleges (*xuéyuàn* 學院) such as College of Liberal Arts (*wén xuéyuàn* 文學院), College of Science (*lǐ xuéyuàn* 理學院), College of Engineering (*gōng xuéyuàn* 工學院), and College of Management (*guǎnlǐ xuéyuàn* 管理學院, the equivalent of School of Business Administration in the United States). For example, in 2022, National Taiwan University (NTU) had a total of 16 colleges and 56 departments, while National Cheng Kung University (NCKU) had 9 colleges and 44 departments. Unlike a US institution, the departments under a College of Liberal Arts in Taiwan are restricted to disciplines like literature, languages, history, philosophy, and anthropology. Political science, sociology, and journalism are all under the College of Social Science. Moreover, universities might categorize certain departments differently. For example, the Department of Psychology is under the College of Science (*lǐ xuéyuàn* 理學院) at NTU, but under the College of Social Sciences at NCKU.

One major difference between the university systems in Taiwan and in the United States is the distribution of the credit hours required for a bachelor's degree among general education and the number of courses required for a major. For instance, an undergraduate student majoring in Chinese needs a minimum of about 128 credit hours to graduate with a BA degree at a semester system university. In the United States, among the 128 credit hours, about 30 credit hours are for major courses, and the rest are mostly counted toward general education. In Taiwan, it is completely opposite. The credit hours for general education are around 30, and the rest are all major-related courses. This example clearly demonstrates the different emphasis in the two higher-education systems. The US system values general education a lot more than the system in Taiwan.

WHY STUDY IN TAIWAN

There are many reasons why students would want to study in Taiwan. First, Taiwan has a friendly environment. Taiwan is a safe, democratic country, and free speech is a basic human right. Students can voice their opinions freely on social media, in public, or in the classroom. No websites are blocked in Taiwan, and people can access Google, Gmail, YouTube, Facebook, and Twitter (or X) directly without relying on a VPN to circumvent government firewalls. Any posts on social media will not be deleted suddenly by government censors. Account holders are solely responsible for their own speech and any consequences.

Diversity

Taiwan is a diverse country whose people love and embrace different cultures. When walking on the streets in Taipei City, you can easily find restaurant and store signs written in different languages such as Korean, Japanese, or English. People in Taiwan especially adore Japanese culture and products. You can find Japanese food, lifestyle goods, and fashion products widespread in Taiwan. Some popular mega department stores in Taiwan even bear Japanese brand names such as Sogo, Mitsukoshi, and Dayeh Takashimaya. When you are inside those department stores, you might feel like you are in Japan.

A Korean food vendor on a university campus. *Image courtesy of Henrietta Yang*

People's enthusiasm about cultural diversity makes Taiwan a very international country. Most younger people in Taiwan learn English quite early, and many can speak English well. Japanese is another popular foreign language that students in Taiwan study at school or learn at *bǔxíbān* (補習班) after school. The food scene on the island also reflects residents' delight in diversity. In food courts on campuses, at train stations, or in shopping malls, you can find a broad array of dishes from different countries, such as Thai noodles, Korean stone bowl rice dishes, Japanese ramen, American burgers, Mexican tacos, and Indian curry. In supermarkets, Japanese, Korean, and American food products are common and abundant. The availability of international products and cuisines will definitely make foreign students' transition into Taiwan easier. According to the Foundation for International Cooperation in Higher Education of Taiwan, there were about 103,658 international students in Taiwan in 2023.[9]

Financial Assistance

Another attractive reason to study in Taiwan is because of the available scholarships and affordable tuition. There are many scholarships and fellowships for international students and scholars offered by Taiwan's government. Here are two useful websites where you can find information about Taiwan fellowships and scholarships:

- https://tafs.mofa.gov.tw/Default.aspx?loc=en
- https://taiwanscholarship.moe.gov.tw/web/pages.aspx?p=7

Mandarin Chinese language learners can apply for *Huayu* Enrichment Scholarship (HES), offered by Taiwan's Ministry of Education (MOE).[10] The duration of study can be during the summer (two months), three months, six months, nine months, or one year, and the monthly stipend is NT$25,000 (around $830). In Taiwan, Mandarin Chinese is called *huáyǔ* (華語) or *guóyǔ* (國語, literally "national language"), while the terms *zhōngwén* (中文) and *hànyǔ* (漢語) are mostly used in Mainland China.

If you are going to Taiwan to study for a degree, there are other scholarships available, such as the MOFA (Ministry of Foreign Affairs) Taiwan Scholarship, the MOE Taiwan Scholarship, and International Higher Education Scholarship Programs. These scholarships provide a tuition waiver, health insurance, and a generous monthly stipend, ranging from NT$15,000 (around $500) to NT$30,000 (around $1,000). In addition, airfare to and from Taiwan are also covered by some scholarships.

For researchers, various financial assistance is also available, including the MOFA Fellowship, MOE Short-Term Research Award (STRA), and Research Grant for Foreign Scholars in Chinese Studies. All these research fellowships provide round-trip airfare and monthly stipends, ranging from NT$25,000 (around $830) for doctoral students to NT$40,000 (around $2,000) for professors. At present, the entry-level salary for a college graduate in Taiwan is around NT$31,000 (around $1,000). Therefore, the monthly stipend provided should be sufficient for comfortable modern living in Taiwan.

If you go to Taiwan to study at your own expense, Taiwan is definitely a good choice because it is safe and affordable. You can expect high-quality education and modern living. According to the Foundation for International Cooperation in Higher Education of Taiwan, in 2023 tuition was between $2,000 and $4,000 per academic year, which is definitely lower than many in-state tuitions in the United States. If you live on campus in Taiwan, room and board costs will normally be between $35 and $284 per month. If you live off campus, the cost will be much higher, around $190 to $570.[11] The difference can be huge based on the location of the university and where you choose to live. For example, the cost of living in Taipei City, the capital of Taiwan, is definitely much higher than other cities. There is also a wide range of rent prices inside Taipei City. Therefore, location is an important factor when students are choosing a university and deciding where to live.

Traditional Chinese Culture

Another good reason for students, especially Chinese language learners, to study in Taiwan is because Taiwan is very traditional, even though it is very international at the same time. Taiwan is a country that has preserved traditional Chinese culture because it did not go through any political movements that denigrated traditional values. Traditional Chinese cultural values are well maintained in Taiwan. People on the island can practice any kind of religion freely. Therefore, temples for Buddhism, Taoism, or Confucianism can be found on major roads or within small alleys. Unlike in China, you do not have to pay to enter any temples in Taiwan. Additionally, Taiwan is the only country in the world still using traditional Chinese characters as the main writing system. Mandarin Chinese learners will be able to appreciate the beauty of this very traditional form of Chinese script everywhere in Taiwan.

A traditional temple in a residential neighborhood. *Image courtesy of Matthew B. Christensen*

Academic Freedom and Faculty Qualification

Lastly, Taiwan respects academic freedom, and faculty qualifications are highly ranked. Academic freedom, like freedom of speech in Taiwan, is observed on every campus, where faculty members, students, and institutions pursue knowledge without government interference. Moreover, more than 80 percent of faculty in universities and colleges hold a PhD degree, and many obtained their highest degrees from the United States or European countries. Therefore, they can relate to international students well and possess cutting-edge knowledge in their fields.

WHERE TO STUDY CHINESE

Taiwan has always been an attractive place to study Chinese. In fact, long before Mainland China became an option for Westerners, Taiwan was *the* place to study Chinese and work in a Mandarin Chinese–speaking environment. In the past decade there has been a renewed interest in Taiwan. This is undoubtedly due to the dramatic increase in the cost of living in the PRC, increasing government regulation and scrutiny of foreigners, the increased political tension between China and the West, and generally, the increasing difficulty of doing business and studying in China in a free and fair way.

For Mandarin Chinese language learners, the major language learning centers are mainly located in Taipei City in the north and in Tainan City and Kaohsiung City in the south of the island. According to Taiwan's Ministry of Education, there are sixty-four Mandarin language centers on the island at present. Twenty-nine of them are located in northern Taiwan, fourteen in central Taiwan, eighteen in southern Taiwan, and three in eastern Taiwan.[12]

The two oldest, largest, and most well-known programs are National Taiwan Normal University's Mandarin Training Center (MTC) and National Taiwan University's International Chinese Language Program (ICLP). MTC was established in 1956 as a center for teaching Chinese to foreigners. It is the largest program in Taiwan, teaching approximately 1,700 students from about eighty different countries per year. ICLP was established in 1962 to cater to the needs of Stanford University students studying Chinese. It has since provided excellent Chinese language training to thousands of students from more than thirty countries. Because of this long history of instruction of Chinese as a foreign language, many other Taiwan universities all over the island also provide excellent Chinese language instruction for foreigners.

When you choose to study Chinese in Taiwan, first you need to decide how long you would like to study—a year or a semester? Or just a summer? Perhaps you are considering pursuing a degree and learning some Chinese along the way. Taiwan's Chinese programs can accommodate all these options.

Summer intensive programs are often an 8-week program, 4 hours a day, 5 days a week. Students will first go through a placement test and be placed in a level that is appropriate for their proficiency level. The language classes are designed to increase not only students' four language skills (reading, listening, speaking, and writing) but also their cultural awareness. Therefore, some culture-related workshops and field trips are generally incorporated into the program. For more advanced students, there are options for taking content courses such as media Chinese and literature courses. Currently, ICLP, MTC, and CET-Taiwan all offer summer intensive programs. The tuition ranges from $8,000 to $9,500, and accommodations cost between $2,000 and $3,500, depending on whether it is a dormitory room or a furnished room in a nice high-rise residential apartment building. Some North American universities also have summer intensive programs affiliated with universities in Taiwan.

A typical semester or yearlong language program offers 15 to 20 hours of language classes per week. MTC and ICLP normally conduct small-size classes and have a wide range of classes for students to choose from. Several of my students participated in an exchange program and studied at the Chinese Language Division in the Language Center of National Taiwan University (NTU) for a semester, which is different from ICLP even though ICLP is also based at NTU. They had 6 hours of Chinese language courses every week and two or three content courses about Taiwan's history and culture, which were taught in English. Obviously, how many hours of Chinese classes you take each week directly affects how fast your Chinese proficiency level improves. Different programs offer different aspects of growth in the language and cultural learning endeavor. Just choose wisely based on what you want to achieve.

Many of the Mandarin language centers mentioned above cater to degree-seeking international students on their own campuses. For example, one of my colleagues used to teach Mandarin Chinese in the International Health Program (IHP) at National Yang Ming University, a medical-based university in Taipei City. The students in her classes were international students pursuing medical degrees at Yang Ming University. However, they needed to learn Mandarin Chinese for survival purposes. Another colleague of mine taught Mandarin Chinese at the language center of National Chung Cheng University in Chiayi for several years. She said that her students, all degree-seeking students, came from many different colleges on campus, such as Business Administration, Finance, Education, Law School, and Engineering. In the academic year 2019–2020, her students came from more than ten different countries, including South Korea, Japan, Thailand, Vietnam, France, India, Germany, Iran, Greece, and Pakistan. The higher-education institutions in Taiwan are extremely accommodating to international students. They will do everything they can to assist international students, such as providing language training courses. Therefore, for degree-seeking students, the most important factors for deciding where to study would be location and scholarship availability.

MAKING THE MOST OF YOUR TIME IN TAIWAN

To many people, studying abroad is a once-in-a-lifetime experience. First, *plan before you go*. As the saying goes: "If you fail to plan, you plan to fail." Even though Taiwan offers modern living and is a safe country, without careful planning you can still run into some mishaps that are certainly avoidable. Therefore, before you go, you should do as much research as you can on Taiwan's climate, living environment, culture, and customs. If you are reading this book, you are on the right track.

When you go to study or work in Taiwan, you are going to spend a much longer time on the island than just a short visit as a tourist. To make your study productive and your stay enjoyable, having a smooth start will make a big difference. For example, if you have a lower tolerance for extreme humidity and hot weather, you might want to avoid arriving in Taiwan during summer, if you have a choice. Taiwan's summer is hot and humid. It is much more pleasant if you go in the spring or winter season, then gradually transition into the summer, rather than diving right into summer's crushing heat with high humidity. If you do not have a choice, then you will want to prepare accordingly. The jeans that many Americans wear daily are not a great idea in the heat of summer. Thin, comfortable clothing, hats, and sunglasses are musts for hot, humid, and muggy weather. When it is time to plan your arrival date, make sure you leave yourself some time before your program starts, because it is crucial to allow yourself to rest properly and get to know the environment before you have to adapt yourself to a new university, which can be stressful.

After you arrive and feel comfortable moving around the university and its neighborhood, keep an open mind and expand your social circle. Try to immerse yourself in the new culture by making friends with locals and other international students. This will quickly expand your understanding of the local culture and broaden your global network. People in Taiwan are generally friendly and warm, and are eager to help foreigners. You can learn a lot of interesting cultural practices from your Taiwanese friends or host families.

> I (Henrietta) can offer an example from my own experience. In my first semester of study in the United States as an undergraduate international student in Southern California, the international student office on campus paired me up with a lovely American family, who invited me to celebrate Thanksgiving with them. I learned so much valuable cultural information that day. For example, I got to know what the "wishbone"

was. In addition, I also encountered two interesting terms that I did not know before: "dark meat" and "white meat." While I tried to use those two terms that day, I made several mistakes by referring to white meat as "light meat." Eventually, I learned that the opposite of "dark meat" was not "light meat," and the opposite of "white meat" was not "black meat." I also learned that a Thanksgiving dinner actually started in the afternoon, not in the evening. What a memorable day! After the first Thanksgiving dinner with my American family twenty-six years ago, we celebrated many more traditional holidays and major milestones in our lives together. A holiday visit turned into a long-lasting friendship, which is one of the most precious experiences in my twenty-six-year life in the United States. The impact of cultural immersion through a caring local family was truly tremendous and unforgettable for an international student.

We have directed and led study abroad programs for American college students for more than twenty-five years. What we have noticed over the years is that the majority of our students tend to stick together when they are abroad, even though we arrange for them language partners or roommates from the local host universities. For those who are willing to step out of their comfort zones and embrace new local friends, their Mandarin Chinese usually improves the most and fastest among all the participants. Moreover, they learn so much useful information from their new friends that they would likely not learn elsewhere. For example, they figure out how to use apps to order delicious food from local restaurants when they don't feel like going out on a rainy day. If you want to make the most of your study or stay, making friends with locals is a must.

To get the most out of your stay in Taiwan, you must go beyond where you stay and explore the island. Traveling in Taiwan is very convenient and manageable. The landscape on the west coast is distinct from the east coast, and foods and cultures in Taipei City are different from those in the south (or central) part of the island. After you have ventured to various parts of the island, you can even explore neighboring countries. Taiwan is situated in a very critical location in East Asia. Visiting a new country is only a few hours away by plane. Within a couple hours, you can easily get to Japan and South Korea in the north, Hong Kong and China in the west, and the Philippines, Thailand, and Vietnam in the south. When my students studied abroad in Taiwan in the summer 2019, several of them went to visit Thailand over a 3-day weekend. They told me that the airfare was extremely cheap, less than $200 for a round-trip ticket!

Studying in Taiwan is safe and fun. Taiwanese are friendly and accommodating, and the academic environment is vibrant and welcoming. There are many financial resources available for foreign students to attend colleges and universities in Taiwan. Just be open-minded and enjoy your experiences, and you will have a fabulous time and develop long-lasting memories.

HOW TO MAKE THE MOST OF YOUR CHINESE LANGUAGE STUDIES

Based on our many years of teaching Chinese as a foreign language and leading study abroad groups, the following tips will help you make the most of your Chinese studies in Taiwan:

- *Make the most of your environment.* Don't spend all day sitting in class and in your room studying. Get out and interact with people. Pay attention to street signs, menus, and so on. Actually being in Taiwan is a great benefit to your language studies. You have an incredibly rich language lab right outside your door. Take every opportunity you can to use and practice your Chinese every day.
- *Practice what you have learned.* Look for ways to use the new vocabulary and grammar you just learned. Listen for it when you are interacting with others. Many young Taiwanese can speak some English and are eager to practice. When you want to practice Chinese, but locals want to speak English with you, you can use an effective trick that one of my students often applied when he studied at a high school in Taiwan. Tell locals that you do not speak English because you are French or German! Just pick a Western country that you like. The chance that locals can speak French or German is much lower than English. This way you do not break the harmony and get to practice your Chinese.
- *Use a notebook or your phone.* Get in the habit of writing down things that you do not understand, so you can later look up words or phrases. Take pictures of characters you don't know. When you encounter a situation you are unfamiliar with, take a few notes, then debrief with a native to learn how to act or what to do in that situation. If you make a mistake, take note so you do not repeat it later.
- *Be a keen observer.* Pay close attention to what is happening around you. If you are not sure what to do in a specific situation, watch

what the Taiwanese locals are doing. For example, if you are not sure how or what to order at a night market, watch what the locals are doing, what they are ordering and how many, how the item is served, and so on. You can learn a great deal by observing locals or those who have been in Taiwan for longer than you.
- *Set goals.* Setting goals will help you gauge your own progress and stay focused on your studies. Goals can be daily, weekly, or monthly. They can be as simple as using a specified number of new vocabulary words each week, or being able to order a meal on your own by the end of the month, or maybe reading a news article each week and talking about it with a local. Be realistic when setting goals, but don't be afraid to push yourself a bit too. Reward yourself when you attain your goals.
- *Be positive and confident.* Setting goals will help you stay focused with your learning. Have a positive attitude and believe in yourself. Learning Chinese is challenging but well within reach of those dedicated to learning it. Don't be too hard on yourself. If you get frustrated (very likely), step back, take a few deep breaths, and dive back in. Stay positive and your chances of good progress will be much better.
- *Utilize your network of friends and colleagues.* Don't be afraid to ask questions. The Taiwanese will be reluctant to correct your mistakes, but if you gently enlist their help (maybe even insist), you can avoid repeated errors and habits that may be hard to change in the future. Your Taiwanese friends and colleagues can play a significant role in your language studies.
- *Hire a tutor.* If your study program does not have outside class help, or if you are interning or working in Taiwan, hiring a tutor can be a fantastic way to improve your language skills. (Sometimes you can arrange a language exchange where you tutor them in English and they help you with your Chinese.) Don't expect this assistance for free. In fact, hiring and paying a tutor has advantages. First, you will be more motivated and serious about your studies and their help; and second, you can set the parameters, discuss what you want to learn, and come up with a plan to accomplish your goals.
- *Embrace the culture.* Do your best to immerse yourself in all aspects of Taiwanese society. Eat local, shop at local markets, make Taiwanese friends and hang out with them. Learn about the local temple in your neighborhood, go to museums, visit national parks, learn about the language of the people where you are living (e.g.,

Taiwanese or Hakka), and learn about the history of the city where you live. Do your best to learn about Taiwanese attitudes toward the West and general world affairs. This may be your one chance to live in Taiwan, so make the most of it.

Table 6.1. Useful Phrases

Teacher	*lǎoshī* (老師)
Professor	*jiàoshòu* (教授)
After-school learning center	*ānqīnbān* (安親班)
Cram school	*bǔxíbān* (補習班), literally "supplementary learning class"
University or college	*dàxué* (大學)
Technological institutes	*kējì dàxué* (科技大學)
National universities	*guólì dàxué* (國立大學)
National technological institutes	*guólì kējì dàxué* (國立科技大學)
Colleges	*xuéyuàn* (學院)
College of Liberal Arts	*wén xuéyuàn* (文學院)
College of Science	*lǐ xuéyuàn* (理學院)
College of Engineering	*gōng xuéyuàn* (工學院)
College of Management	*guǎnlǐ xuéyuàn* (管理學院)
Mandarin Chinese	*huáyǔ* (華語), *guóyǔ* (國語), literally "national language" in Taiwan
Mandarin Chinese	*zhōngwén* (中文), *hànyǔ* (漢語), in Mainland China

7

WORKING AND INTERNING IN TAIWAN

Taiwan is an international country with free markets. Many well-known global corporations have branches in Taiwan, such as Carrefour (French), IKEA (Swedish), Alcon (American Swiss), and Deloitte, Starbucks, and Costco (American). Some well-known global corporations are originally from Taiwan, such as Taiwan Semiconductor (the world's most valuable semiconductor company) and Foxconn (Hon Hai Technology Group). This chapter will help you learn how to find an internship or a job in

A Costco store in New Taipei City. *Image courtesy of Henrietta Yang*

TSMC buildings inside Hsinchu Science Park. *Image courtesy of Henrietta Yang*

Taiwan and how to be successful at your job. Knowing Taiwanese business culture is crucial.

HOW TO LAND AN INTERNSHIP OR JOB

There are three major ways of getting an internship or a job in Taiwan: (1) through a partnership between a corporation and an academic entity, (2) through online hiring platforms or a company's website, and (3) through connections (*guānxì* 關係).

Industry-Academic Collaboration

When a corporation or organization collaborates with an academic unit (be it a department or an individual professor), it is called *chǎnxué hézuò* (產學合作, literally "industry-academic collaboration"). There are various ways to collaborate, but the goal is the same: to produce students who are more prepared for a specific industry's needs. Under this type of partnership, students will take some specific courses related to an industry during the regular semesters and do an internship during summer and winter breaks. Most of these kinds of internships are in STEM and medical fields. For example, UMC (United Microelectronics Corporation 聯華電子), a semiconductor company, collaborates with several national universities and technical colleges in Taiwan such as National Tsing Hua University, National Chiao Tung University, National Cheng Kung University, and

UMC buildings inside Hsinchu Science Park. *Image courtesy of Henrietta Yang*

National Central University.[1] This strategy helps big corporations secure job candidates much earlier, since the competition for STEM graduates in Taiwan is intense. UMC, for example, is able to hire 100 to 200 graduates from *chǎnxué hézuò* (產學合作) programs every year. If you plan to study in Taiwan and are a degree-seeking student, you might want to find an institution that has collaborations in the fields you are interested in. That will be the easiest way of getting an internship in the future, and perhaps a job after you graduate.

The internship and job situation in Taiwan is similar to that in the United States. For a STEM student, as the Chinese saying goes, it is 事求人 *shì qiú rén* (literally "work begs people"), meaning companies are begging/searching for people who can do the job. Jobs or internships in the STEM fields are consistently available, and the monthly salary is around NT$50,000 or above (about $1,600). However, it is the other way around for a student studying in traditional liberal arts majors. It is 人求事 *rén qiú shì* (literally "people beg work"), meaning it is people who are begging/searching for jobs. The job market is much more competitive in liberal arts fields, but the pay is not necessarily higher. The monthly salary for a college graduate with a degree in liberal arts is around NT$35,000 (about $1,200) or so.

Job-Searching Websites

In addition to institutions' connections with corporations, students can also look for internship or job opportunities via Taiwan's major hiring platforms. These include Taiwan's LinkedIn, 1111 Human Power Bank, and 104 Human Power Bank.

TAIWAN'S LINKEDIN[2]

This is a Chinese version of LinkedIn that is used in Taiwan. Jobs are posted in either English or Chinese in traditional characters. When I visited the website (August 24, 2022), there were 11,000 job openings. Like any job search engine, you can filter your search based on a specific company, location, and/or types of positions.

When searching for an internship, just select 實習機會 (*shíxí jīhuì*, internship opportunity) under 職階等級 (*zhíjiē děngjí*, rank levels). After selecting 實習機會 (*shíxí jīhuì*, internship opportunity) and clicking 完成 (*wánchéng*, finish), you will see a list of internship opportunities (118 openings when I visited the page). It should be very intuitive for Generation Z to navigate a site like this.

1111 人力銀行 (1111 *RÉNLÌ YÍNHÁNG*, 1111 HUMAN POWER BANK)[3]

On this site, you can search jobs as well as internship opportunities. Like LinkedIn, you can search jobs based on certain preferences such as remote work, monthly salary (e.g., NT$40,000 and above), or 5 workdays only. This site not only provides a job search engine but also includes many useful resources and services for first-time job seekers, such as samples of résumés, and provides professional suggestions, how to prepare for interviews, and frequent interview questions. It is beneficial for American students to take a look and compare the business cultural differences between the United States and Taiwan.

On this site, there is a link to TUN 大學網 (*dàxué wǎng*, "college websites"),[4] which is specifically for college students who are freshmen or are preparing to enter the job market. It contains a great deal of useful information. For example, under 全國大學 (*quánguó dàxué*, "all colleges and universities in Taiwan"), you can find information about specific departments and universities as well as scholarship options from each university.

Moreover, under 認識職涯 (*rènshi zhíyá*, "get to know job markets"), there is information about salary ranges for different jobs and tips for new job hunters. 職涯導航 (*zhíyá dǎoháng*, "career guidance") includes details about internship opportunities and job definitions. All this information is helpful to college students who are preparing themselves for entering the job market.

In addition, under 新生必看 (xīnshēng bìkàn, "freshmen must read"), there is useful information for freshmen such as specifics about academic departments and dorms and apartments.

104 人力銀行 (104 *RÉNLÌ YÍNHÁNG*, 104 HUMAN POWER BANK)[5]

On this site, there are similar filters to narrow down job listings based on salary ranges, work hours, specific skills, and so forth. One practical feature on this platform is that it offers specific pages for job searchers at different stages of their life or career, such as students (學生 *xuésheng*), new graduates (新鮮人 *xīnxiān rén*), current employees thinking of changing jobs (上班族 *shàngbān zú*), supervisor-level or advanced positions (主管職 *zhǔguǎn zhí*), and positions for middle-aged and senior people. Take the students' page, for example; it lists mainly internship and part-time work opportunities since those job opportunities are more practical to students than to senior level job seekers. Other functions on this site are similar to the other two sites discussed previously.

Since these websites are only in Chinese characters, unless you have high-level Chinese language skills, you may need to enlist the help of a native to navigate these sites.

Through Connections (guānxī 關係)

Another way of getting an internship or a job is through connections (*guānxī* 關係), which play an important role in Chinese and Taiwanese societies. Normally, connections (*guānxī* 關係) are built up gradually, made through networks over time. For foreign students, your professors—either at your home institutions in the United States or at the university you attend in Taiwan—might be key persons who can help you start your *guānxī* network in Taiwan based on their connections with people in Taiwan. Therefore, it is crucial to treat your instructors with respect and to interact with them appropriately based on cultural norms. In Taiwan's culture, Taiwanese might not let foreigners or foreign students know when they are offended. They will just avoid you in the future.

TAIWANESE BUSINESS CULTURE

Taiwan is an international country with free markets, and many countries have established branches of their companies on the island. The business culture you will encounter depends on what kind of company you work for, and your experience might vary slightly depending on where you work. In addition, for students who have worked in China in the past, do not assume the culture you encountered in Mainland China can be directly transferred to Taiwan's business settings.

In Taiwan, work hours can vary from company to company. Taiwan's business culture used to be heavily influenced by Japanese culture, which values long working hours in the office. It used to be very rare for employees to clock out punctually. Long working hours were seen as dedication, devotion, and commitment to the company. However, nowadays some companies in Taiwan, especially those corporations from Western countries, have shifted from valuing long work hours to valuing work efficiency. However, Japanese and Taiwanese companies still expect longer working hours than in the West.

In a normal business work space, only high-ranking officers have their own office. Most employees are assigned open cubicles. It is best to keep your space organized and clean, even though it is your own personal space. In addition, control your volume when you speak on the phone. Being mindful of how your "neighbors" feel is another way of showing respect.

Teamwork and workplace harmony are two important components of business culture in Taiwan. American culture values individualism. However, the working culture in Taiwan values teamwork and harmonious working relationships among employees. One way of maintaining harmony at work is by respecting seniority and rank, because hierarchy is crucial in Chinese culture. To show respect, it is important to know how to appropriately address your colleagues who are more senior than you and those who hold higher ranks than you. A rule of thumb is not to address your colleagues by their first names in Chinese when you meet them for the first time. Always address people by their last names, followed by appropriate titles such as Miss *xiǎojiě* (小姐) or Ms. *nǚshì* (女士), Mr. *xiānshēng* (先生), director *zhǔrèn* (主任), manager *jīnglǐ* (經理), and chairman *dǒngshìzhǎng* (董事長). For example, if you meet a gentleman who introduces himself as "我姓王 (My surname is Wang)," but you do not know his rank, then you should greet him as "*wáng xiānshēng* (王先生, Mr. Wang)" and politely ask for his business card to figure out what to call him based on his rank. If you find out he is a manager, then you should call him "Wang *jīnglǐ* (王經理)" unless he insists that you call him something else.

Many Taiwanese people have English names, which many use in the workplace. Calling one another by English names does not permit you to call them by their first names in Chinese. This is a delicate balance. For Taiwanese, their first names in Chinese are reserved for family and close friends. Until they say, "You can call me [first name in Chinese]," do not use their first names in Chinese.

Some senior colleagues or managers might address young colleagues by adding *xiǎo* (小 "small, young") in front of their last name to show friendliness, cordiality, affection, or intimacy—for example, *xiǎo* Wang (小王)—but that does not imply that you can address your senior colleagues by adding the opposite of *xiǎo* (小 "small, young"), *lǎo* (老 "old"), in front of their last name, such as *lǎo* Chen (老陳), even though other senior colleagues might already address each other that way. Again, this is a delicate balance. It is always best to choose a polite and formal approach in the beginning.

In addition to addressing your colleagues or clients appropriately, your body language is equally important. In Taiwan, when you meet someone for the first time, you can either nod your head to acknowledge or shake hands, depending on the situation. When you shake hands with someone you meet for the first time, do not offer a strong, firm handshake. Unlike the American custom, a handshake in Taiwan is usually done by softly touching each other's hands. If a handshake is not convenient due to the distance, then look at the person you are introduced to and nod your head slightly to acknowledge their presence. A hug is appropriate only after people get to know you well. In general, people do not hug each other at the first business meeting, and sometimes not at all.

To work as a team, people must communicate with each other and make decisions based on the majority's direction. However, usually it is high-ranking supervisors who have the final say. The way Taiwanese express their ideas and thoughts tends to be indirect. Direct opinions are considered strong and aggressive, which can hurt the workplace harmony. It will take foreigners some time to be able to read between the lines. For example, when you invite a Taiwanese coworker to have dinner, they might say, "Okay, let me check my schedule and see if that works." That colleague probably will not follow up because that is their indirect way of saying "No." Saying no directly to people is seen as too harsh and not nice, and may cause a loss of face.

The "face" issue (*miànzi* 面子) is deeply embedded into every aspect of people's life in Taiwan. For example, when children get into top national universities, their parents gain or have "face" (*yǒu miànzi* 有面子). If you were to reject someone's gift in public, you cause that person to lose "face" (*méiyǒu miànzi* 沒有面子). In the workplace, if a boss invites you to a dinner and you decline the offer in public, you are not giving him "face" (*bù gěi miànzi* 不給面子). If you invited colleagues to dinner, but did not order enough dishes, this would cause you to lose face. On the other hand, if you ordered more than what your guests can consume, then you have face.

Many newlyweds roll out lavish weddings to make their parents have face. In the workplace, how to balance your actions and give colleagues face to maintain workplace harmony is an art.

The language of communication at many workplaces in Taiwan is mostly Chinese, but Taiwanese is also used quite often, especially in the south. Learning some Taiwanese before you travel will go a long way in establishing trust and getting along with your colleagues. Another characteristic feature of Taiwanese communication is code-switching—mixing different languages when speaking. Sometimes, it happens even within one sentence. It is quite common to mix Taiwanese and Chinese or Chinese and English when speaking. Sometimes, even some Japanese vocabulary might slip into a sentence.

For students who previously studied or worked in Mainland China, you will quickly notice that the communication styles and word choices in Taiwan can be very different from those in China. A friend of mine (Henrietta), who has worked in human resources for more than twenty-five years in both China and Taiwan, compared the communication differences. He said, "People are much more direct in China, while Taiwanese are much more indirect, so they don't break the harmonious working relationship." He also mentioned that in China, workers clock out when it's time. They also take breaks and have lunch promptly. In Taiwan, employees mostly put work first, and lunch and breaks second. So they often work overtime.

During a conversation, Taiwanese usually provide some conversational cues to let listeners know they are listening, such as "哦，是哦" (*o, shì o*, "oh, I see"), "這樣啊" (*zhèyàng ā*, "oh, I see"), "嗯" (*ēng*, "uh-huh"), and "好啊" (*hǎo ā*, "okay"), and nod occasionally to indicate interest while listening.

Office dress code: The rule of thumb of how to dress appropriately in the workplace is to go with business professional first, then adjust based on the office culture. For example, if your internship is at a technology company and everyone goes to work in business casual, then you should change from a business professional dress code to business casual. On the other hand, if your colleagues all wear a shirt and tie to work, then you should do the same. In Taiwan, summer is extremely long, hot, and humid. It is common for men to wear short-sleeved dress shirts in summer, which are made of lighter, breathable fabrics. That type of clothing is not as common in American workplaces. If you are going to study or work in Taiwan, you can wait and buy clothing from local department stores after you settle in. For women, office dresses should not be too tight or revealing. It is also common for women to wear only light makeup.

STRATEGIES TO MAKE THE MOST OF YOUR WORK/INTERNSHIP

To make the most of your work or study experience in Taiwan, we have three suggestions: First, learn some languages (Chinese and Taiwanese) and as much culture as possible. Even though many Taiwanese can speak English, knowing some local languages will help you navigate around the island better. Most Taiwanese are very friendly, and will help you whether you speak the language or not. But knowing some local languages will help you connect better to your colleagues and make your stay more enjoyable. Learning a language takes time, but you should read more about Taiwanese culture as soon as possible. Even if you cannot speak Chinese or Taiwanese, but you can interact with locals appropriately, you will definitely be well received.

Second, actively participate in events on campus or at work. The cultures on campus and at the workplace value teamwork. Participating in university or company events can extend your network and broaden your connections (*guānxi* 關係) beyond your work unit or academic major.

Third, be open-minded and try to understand how Taiwanese think and what they value, such as "face" issues, indirectness, family values, and food culture. As the proverb goes: "When in Rome, do as the Romans do." Examples include the Taiwanese custom of wearing indoor slippers (mentioned in chapter 5), the dining custom of not serving or drinking cold water with a meal (see chapter 4), and the tradition of children staying at home until they get married (see chapter 6). You will have a fun time during your stay if you are willing to embrace and adapt to Taiwanese customs and way of life.

The working environment in Taiwan is friendly and safe. Overall, Taiwan offers convenient transportation systems, an excellent low-cost health-care system, fabulous food, a relatively low cost of living, and hospitable residents. If you have an opportunity to work in Taiwan, it will be a memorable experience.

Table 7.1. Useful Phrases

關係	*guānxī* (connections)
產學合作	*chǎnxué hézuò* (industry-academic collaboration)
實習機會	*shíxí jīhuì* (internship opportunity)
人力銀行	*rénlì yínháng* (human power bank)
職階等級	*zhíjiē děngjí* (rank levels)
學生	*xuéshēng* (students)
新鮮人	*xīnxiān rén* (new graduates)
上班族	*shàngbān zú* (current employees)
主管職	*zhǔguǎn zhí* (supervisor-level or advanced positions)
小姐	*xiǎojiě* (Miss)
女士	*nǚshì* (Ms.)
先生	*xiānshēng* (Mr.)
主任	*zhǔrèn* (director)
經理	*jīnglǐ* (manager)
董事長	*dǒngshìzhǎng* (chairman)
小	*xiǎo* (small, young)
老	*lǎo* (old, senior)
面子	*miànzi* ("face")
有面子	*yǒu miànzi* (to have "face")
沒有面子	*méiyǒu miànzi* (to lose "face")
不給面子	*bù gěi miànzi* (not giving someone "face")
哦，是哦	*o, shì o* (Oh, I see)
這樣啊	*zhèyàng ā* (Oh, I see)
嗯	*ēng* (uh-huh)
好啊	*hǎo ā* (okay)

8

TAIWAN'S DIVERSE GEOGRAPHY

Though Taiwan is a small island, it is incredibly diverse. In its simplest form, Taiwan can be divided into east, west, north, and south. Each of the four regions of the island has its own industries, culture, languages, and overall feeling or vibe. West and east are separated by the Central Mountain Range. The west, from Taipei in the north, all the way down to Kaohsiung in the south, is where the vast majority of Taiwan's people live. It is composed of sloping flatlands from the mountains to the sea. It is also where most of the industries, universities, and large cities are located. The east side of Taiwan comprises about 20 percent of the land, but only 3 percent of the population. It contains rich agricultural valleys, rice paddies, and rugged coastline with beaches and resorts. With Taiwan's excellent public transportation systems, it is quite convenient to get anywhere on the island without much trouble. You can also drive just about anywhere in a matter of hours.

There are a number of excellent guidebooks on the market where you can get specific suggestions on what to see, where to go, and what to do in each of these regions, complete with addresses, phone numbers, and other information. We do not attempt to duplicate that information here. Instead, we provide more general information about each region, how they are unique, the predominant industries, and the people, languages, and cultural identities of these varied places. For example, in the United States, the southern states have different culture, food, and attitudes from the Northeast or the West or the Midwest. Though Taiwan may be a bit more homogeneous than the United States, different regions of Taiwan do have a different feel, with different food specialties, languages spoken, and varying attitudes of the people in these areas.

In this chapter we provide background information about each of the four regions of Taiwan. Here is a simplified glance at Taiwan's four main regions, centered on the central city or cities of that region.

North (Taipei, *táiběi* 台北): Big-city life, the political, business, and commercial center of Taiwan. Taipei is the capital of Taiwan. The character 北 (*běi*) in Taipei's Chinese name, 台北, means "north," and the city's name can be understood as in the north of Taiwan.

West (Taichung, *táizhōng* 台中): Manufacturing and industrial heartland in the west. Like Taipei, Taichung's Chinese name also indicates its geographic location on the island. The Chinese character 中 (*zhōng*) in 台中 means "middle," and its name can be understood as in the middle of Taiwan. Since the west is where the majority of businesses and people are, the middle here refers to the "middle" in the western part of Taiwan.

South (Tainan, *táinán* 台南 and Kaohsiung, *gāoxióng* 高雄): The cultural and historical center of Taiwan, and the major import/export shipping hub. Like Taipei 台北 and Taichung 台中, the Chinese name of Tainan, 台南, can be seen as in the south of Taiwan because 南 (*nán*) means "south."

East (Hualien, *huālián* 花蓮 and Taitung, *táidōng* 台東): Scenic beauty, agricultural, and ethnic minorities. 東 (*dōng*) means "east"; therefore, 台東 can be understood as Taiwan's east.

TAIPEI AND NORTHERN TAIWAN

Taipei is the political, business, and commercial center of Taiwan. When most people fly to Taiwan, they arrive at the big international airport in Taoyuan, a short distance from central Taipei. This is also the most densely populated area of Taiwan, with a population around 7 million. This includes New Taipei City (*xīnběi shì* 新北市) and other surrounding areas, which used to be zoned under the name Taipei County (*táiběi xiàn* 台北縣). It really is one big metropolis. When most people refer to Taipei, in general, they are talking about the surrounding metropolitan areas as well. Just like in the United States, when we refer to Los Angeles we generally mean the whole LA suburban area. However, when locals talk about where they live in Taipei, they will use the name of their district, such as 中和 (*zhōnghé*), 板橋 (*bǎnqiáo*), and 新莊 (*xīnzhuāng*). Even people who live in Taipei City, which has about 10 percent of the country's population, will do the same—for example, 天母 (*tiānmǔ*), 士林 (*shìlín*), 木柵 (*mùzhà*), and 萬華 (*wànhuá*). For foreigners who are in Taiwan for a longer visit, it is beneficial to know the names of the different districts.

Taiwan's Diverse Geography   137

Taipei's skyline. *Image courtesy of Henrietta Yang*

The Greater Taipei area is home to countless restaurants, night markets, shopping centers, museums, universities, historic sites, and so on. Many people who visit Taiwan never leave the Taipei area and still have a memorable experience. Though the Taipei area is urban, it is surrounded by mountains, countryside, natural hot springs, and easy access to the northern coast.

Taipei's most iconic site is Taipei 101, the 101-story skyscraper that resembles bamboo. The building was completed on December 31, 2004, and was the world's tallest building until January 2010. There is a luxury atrium-type shopping mall on the lowest floors, with offices taking up most of the remaining floors. An indoor observation deck is on the 89th floor and an outdoor one on the 91st floor. There are also numerous restaurants, clubs, and other facilities in the building.

Taipei 101. *Image courtesy of Henrietta Yang*

The Taipei area is also the place for fashion and shopping. Shi-men Ting (西門町, xīméndīng) in western Taipei City in the Wanhua District (萬華區, wànhuá qū) is one of the best places to go for young people looking for trendy clothing and accessories. Xinyi District (信義區, xìnyì qū) in eastern Taipei caters to shopaholics looking for more high-end luxury goods. I (Henrietta) love shopping and am particularly interested in Taiwan's 文創商品 (wénchuàng shàngpǐn), hugely popular in the past decade in Taiwan. 文創商品 (wénchuàng shàngpǐn) refers to culturally innovated products, which are fun and creative. Some amuse me because of the extension and application of a certain cultural aspect, and others are just purely artistic and innovative. Several places in the heart of Taipei City, such as Songshan Cultural and Creative Park (松山文創園區, sōngshān wénchuàng yuánqū) and Huashan 1914 Creative Park (華山 1914 文化創意產業園區, huáshān 1914 wénhuà chuàngyì chǎnyè yuánqū), are paradises for me when it comes to creative cultural products.

In addition to excellent Chinese cuisine, you can also find outstanding international and fusion cuisines in Taipei. In fact, Taiwan has twenty-six Michelin-starred restaurants. The only other Taiwan city with Michelin-starred restaurants is Taichung with four.[1] Taipei has been justifiably called a foodie's paradise, and contends for best city in Asia for eating out.

The Taipei area has everything—great food, night markets, every level of accommodation from five-star luxury hotels to youth hostels, several excellent universities, museums, cultural sights, and more. It also makes a good base to see other parts of Taiwan. As mentioned in chapter 3 on travel, Taipei is a hub for travel to just about any other place in Taiwan. Trains, subways, buses, and bikeshare bicycles are all available in the Taipei area.

North of Taipei are three places worth visiting. One is Tamshui (淡水, dànshuǐ), at the end of the Red Line MRT. Though this was originally a sleepy fishing village, it is now a lively town on the coast with a nice night market, Tamkang University (淡江大學, dànjiāng dàxué), and pleasant open spaces along the shoreline to walk or picnic. It's a mere 45 minutes away from central Taipei. The other two are Keelung (基隆, jīlóng) and Jiufen (九份, jiǔfèn). Keelung is a good-size city north of Taipei, conveniently accessible by train or bus in only about 40 minutes. Keelung has a famous and quite large night market that specializes in seafood because of its proximity to the ocean, and is a major port in Taiwan. Jiufen is a small village on the mountainside above the coast. It used to be a prosperous town because of its gold and coal mines in the late nineteenth century. Now it has been transformed into lively markets and shopping in the old town area, but is most known for the terraced buildings built on the mountainside. It is said that the famous Japanese anime director Hayao Miyazaki used this town as the inspiration for the town in the animated film *Spirited Away*. Getting to Jiufen is a little more complicated, requiring an 80-minute train ride, then a 10-minute bus ride. It is more convenient if you take an Uber or drive yourself.

Other things to see and do in Taipei include the National Palace Museum (故宮博物院, *gùgōng bówùyuàn*), hot springs in Beitou (北投, *běitóu*) or Yangming Mountain (陽明山, *yángmíng shān*), Yingge ceramic old town (鶯歌陶瓷老街, *yīnggē táocí lǎojiē*), and Shifen (十分, *shífēn*) for making and flying your own sky lantern.

The other major city in the northern part of Taiwan is Hsinchu (新竹, *xīnzhú*), about 45 miles southwest of Taipei. This city is well known for its science park, which is considered the Silicon Valley of Taiwan. Many semiconductor manufacturers have their headquarters, large offices, and factories here. Because of these advanced technology companies and two premium national universities—Tsinghua and Yangming-Jiaotong (國立清華大學, *guólì qīnghuá dàxué* and 國立陽明交通大學, *guólì yángmíng jiāotōng dàxué*)—the housing market in the Hsinchu area has become one of the most expensive in Taiwan.

Before young STEM professionals moved to Hsinchu, the majority of the population was Hakka. Therefore, you can find a great deal of authentic Hakka cuisines there. For students who are looking for internships, Hsinchu is a city that offers a wide variety of opportunities, from STEM areas to business.

TAICHUNG AND WESTERN TAIWAN

When you think about the western side of central Taiwan, you usually think about Taichung City, Taichung Harbor, and industry. For instance, many big semiconductor companies have factories in this part of Taiwan, Taiwan Semiconductor Manufacturing Company (TSMC) being the largest. In fact, Taiwan is the leading chip manufacturer in the world, with more than 60 percent by revenue.[2] The Taichung and Hsinchu areas truly are the Taiwan equivalent of Silicon Valley. There is a great deal of not only high-tech companies, but also manufacturing enterprises, from bicycles to car parts and everything in between. In addition to the big manufacturing companies in Taiwan like Giant Bicycles and Foxconn Technology Group (maker of the Apple iPhone), one thing a little different about Taiwan manufacturing is that many of the companies are small family-run operations, or at least started that way. Many successful companies prefer

Sun Moon Lake. *Image courtesy of Henrietta Yang*

to hand down the company to family members rather than sell to private equity investors or bank investors, even though sometimes their companies are worth a great deal.

Although this region of Taiwan is the center of industry, there is a great deal of diversity here as well. Geographically, western Taiwan is sandwiched between the high Central Mountain Range and the coast. In Taichung, there is the Gaomei Wetland Preservation Area (高美濕地, *gāoměi shīdì*), and mountain resorts at Nantou's Sun Moon Lake (日月潭, *rìyuètán*) and Chiayi's Alishan National Scenic Area (阿里山國家森林遊樂區, *ālǐshān guójiā sēnlín yóulèqū*).

The largest city in this region is Taichung (台中, *tāizhōng*), literally Taiwan's "middle" or central, which is the second-largest city in Taiwan. Being centrally located on the island, it only takes a little more than 1 hour to go from central Taipei City to Taichung via high-speed trains, and another hour to the largest city in the south, Kaohsiung (高雄, *gāoxióng*). Taichung is also a seaport city. On the west coast of the city is the second-largest container shipping port in Taiwan.

Taichung is also home to several universities, such as National Chung Hsing University (國立中興大學, *guólì zhōngxīng dàxué*), Feng Chia University (逢甲大學, *féngjiǎ dàxué*), and Tunghai University (東海大學, *dōnghǎi dàxué*). Because of its convenient transportation system and talented college graduates, Taichung, like Hsinchu, also has a science park, which hosts many semiconductor factories.

In addition to Taichung, another important city in this region is Chiayi (嘉義, *jīayì*), which is a gateway city to Alishan (阿里山, *ālǐshān*). It is also an important historical city, dating back to the seventeenth century. Nowadays, Chiayi is a dynamic agricultural region for fruits, vegetables,

Pineapple fields in Minxiong. *Image courtesy of Matthew B. Christensen*

rice, and grains. Pineapples, which are the essential ingredient for Taiwan's famous pineapple cakes (鳳梨酥, *fènglí sū*), are one of the major agricultural products in this region.

When I (Henrietta) was searching for a university partner in Taiwan to host a summer program for my students, I decided to work with National Chung Cheng University (國立中正大學, *guólì zhōngzhèng dàxué*), which is located in Minxiong (民雄, *mínxióng*) Township, Chiayi County. The university is surrounded by many pineapple fields, and there is a pineapple factory and a visitor center nearby that my students and colleagues found very interesting and unique. You can buy freshly made pineapple cakes and delicious pineapples straight from the farm behind the visitor center if you visit in the right season. There are also many interesting pineapple products such as pineapple juice, ice cream, vinegar, and tea.

HUALIEN AND EASTERN TAIWAN

Taiwan's east coast, from Yilan (宜蘭, *yílán*) in the north to Taitung (台東, *táidōng*) in the south, is dotted with small farming and fishing villages, rice paddies, rugged mountains and gorges, beautiful beaches, and a slower pace of life compared to the rest of Taiwan. The three largest cities in eastern Taiwan, Yilan (宜蘭, *yílán*), Hualien (花蓮, *huālián*), and Taitung (台東, *táidōng*) have most of what other Taiwanese cities have—night markets, shopping districts, hotels, and business centers—but on a much smaller scale. For example, the night market in Hualien might be a bit of a disappointment compared to the massive markets in the Taipei area. Though it is rather small, it is quaint, with some specialties you won't find easily in other parts of Taiwan.

The east is where you go when you want to get away from the big cities. The climate on the east coast is somewhat drier than on the north and west sides of Taiwan, making it a bit more comfortable. However, the east also gets the brunt of the yearly cycle of typhoons that can hammer the coast with heavy rain and wind. The east also has a bit more seismic activity as well.

If you come from small-town America, Yilan (population 455,000), Hualien (population 106,000), and Taitung (population 107,000) might seem big with their tall buildings, traffic, and other infrastructure, but compared to Taiwan's other cities, they are small and picturesque, considering Taipei's 2.6 million and Taichung's 2.8 million residents. It is all relative, and Taiwan's east coast has a smaller-town feel where life is not quite as fast-paced and hectic, which is why the east coast is a popular vacation choice for residents living on the west coast. The people on the east

Coastal cliffs in Hualien. *Image courtesy of Matthew B. Christensen*

coast seem a bit more laid-back as well. You can still find all the modern conveniences you might need, but you will not have the same variety and number of options as in bigger cities.

Taiwan's east is home to the largest number of aboriginal groups. Though many of these people have assimilated with Taiwanese, they do retain their distinct languages, cultures, dress, and customs. Many still live in remote villages, so you may hear different languages spoken in this part of Taiwan, aboriginal as well as Taiwanese.

Taiwan's biggest aboriginal group is called Amis (阿美族, *āměi zú*), with a population of 213,514. They mainly reside between Hualien and Taitung and constitute the third-largest ethnic group on the island. Another smaller tribe, Bunun (布農族, *bùnóng zú*), with a population of 59,536, has about one-third living in this region as well. Some aboriginal groups do not spread that widely. For example, Puyuma (卑南族, *bēinán zú*) and Rukai (魯凱族, *lǔkǎi zú*) mainly reside in Taitung County; their populations are both around 14,000. In addition, about two-thirds of the 32,333 Truku members (太魯閣族, *tàilǔgé zú*) live in the Hualien region. Moving farther north, you can find Kavalan (噶瑪蘭族, *gámǎlán zú*) and Atayal (泰雅族, *tàiyǎ zú*) in the Yilan region. Atayal's population is around 92,084, but only 12,500 members of the tribe reside in the Yilan area; the rest are scattered throughout the island. Kavalan is a fairly small group, whose population is only around 1,500.[3] The east coast of Taiwan is an exciting region that not only provides very different scenery from the west coast, but also presents a wide range of indigenous cultures.

While there are smaller temples in the area to visit, the main reason for coming to the east coast is the scenic beauty. One of these sights is the famous Taroko Gorge National Park (太魯閣國家公園, *tàilǔgé guójiā gōngyuán*). This beautiful gorge, or canyon, is a short distance from Hualien and is a major tourist site in Taiwan. The lower Liwu River has carved a magnificent canyon through walls of marble. It is quite impressive to see sheer walls of polished marble and huge marble boulders scattered throughout the canyon.

Most people join large tour groups and are bussed up to the gorge. The last time I (Matt) was there, I rented a scooter in Hualien and rode about 45 minutes up into the gorge. I much preferred this way as I could wander about wherever I wanted and didn't have to wait for a group. If you are the kind that likes to explore on your own, this is a good way to go. Of course, if you have a car you can drive there yourself and see things on your own terms, too. However, parking will be an issue in many of

Taroko Gorge National Park near Hualien. *Image courtesy of Matthew B. Christensen*

the scenic spots along the main road. There are numerous waterfalls, scenic hikes, and temples throughout the gorge.

All along the east coast there are numerous waterfalls, hot springs, beaches, and quiet country roads to explore. Chishang (池上, *chíshàng*), in the northern part of Taitung County, is where you will find organic rice farming. Because of the high quality of rice, Chishang's lunch boxes (便當, *biàndāng*) have become very famous and popular on the island. Many tourists go all the way to Chishang just to taste the rice or lunch boxes there. Taitung City on the islands' southeast coast is the southern terminus of scenic coastal Highway 11. This region is famous for fresh fruit, especially wax apples (蓮霧, *liánwù*). In additional to agricultural products, Chihpen (知本, *zhīběn*) in Taitung City is well known for hot springs, a popular tourist site for residents on the island.

The major city on the northern end of the east coast is Yilan (宜蘭, *yílán*), situated in the northeast corner of the island. Its major industries are tourism and agriculture. For instance, Yilan's Jiaoxi (礁溪, *jiāoxī*) is famous for hot springs, and there are many hot springs resorts in this area. From Taipei Station, it is only a 50-minute drive to Jiaoxi, about 30 miles. Another important site in Yilan is called Su'ao (蘇澳, *sūào*), which is a town on the Pacific Ocean. Because of its location, it is an important naval base as well as fishing port. The seafood is famous here. When a region has excellent seafood and hot springs, and is not far from Taipei City, many residents in Taipei often take a day trip to Yilan to enjoy the relaxing hot springs and delicious, fresh seafood.

For outdoor enthusiasts, Taiwan's east coast is a paradise. The huge playground accommodates activities like camping, hiking, kayaking, rafting, surfing, diving, and fishing. Cycling is also popular on Taiwan's east coast and includes the Taiwan Cycling Route 1, which goes all the way around the island and is 968 kilometers (600 miles). There are numerous other excellent bicycle routes along quiet country roads through Taiwan's Rift Valley, inland along Highway 9 and other less traveled roads.

TAINAN, KAOHSIUNG, AND SOUTHERN TAIWAN

Some would argue that the southern part of Taiwan, particularly the city of Tainan (台南, *táinán*), is the heart of traditional Taiwanese culture. There are sound arguments that can be made to support this. Tainan is where the first immigrants from the Chinese Mainland settled in Taiwan back in the seventeenth century, and it was the first capital. They say if you want to see and experience traditional Taiwanese culture, go to Tainan. You will also notice that there is a lot of Taiwanese (台語, *táiyǔ*, also known as Hokkien) spoken in public. In fact, the percentage of speakers of Taiwanese as their dominant language is higher in southern Taiwan than anywhere else on the island. Most of my (Matt) colleagues and acquaintances from southern Taiwan all speak Taiwanese fluently. In fact, most grew up speaking Taiwanese in their homes with their parents and siblings. Further evidence of this fact can be seen with political candidates. It is imperative that candidates campaigning for political office speak Taiwanese at rallies and other political functions. This assures the people in southern Taiwan that their candidate is one of them.

As a foreigner in Taiwan, if you speak Mandarin Chinese, you will get around just fine. All educated individuals in Taiwan are fluent in Mandarin, even if they grew up speaking Taiwanese as their first language. Mandarin is the primary language spoken in school and has been the official language of Taiwan since 1945. However, you might experience heavier Taiwanese accents when locals in the south speak Mandarin Chinese.

Most of Tainan's cultural and historical attractions are clustered in the center of the city around the Anping Old Fort area (安平古堡, *ānpíng gǔbǎo*), which was built by the Dutch from 1624 to 1634. This makes it easy to walk around and explore this very interesting city. The most well-known street in the historic city center is Anping Old Street (安平老街, *ānpíng lǎojiē*), which is packed with small eateries serving traditional local dishes. My (Henrietta) favorite dishes on the Old Street from my last visit were fried shrimp wontons (炸蝦仁餛飩, *zhà xiārén húntún*), oyster omelet with a savory sauce (蚵仔煎, *kēzǎijiān*), and tofu pudding/soybean pudding with peanuts in a sweet ginger syrup (花生豆花, *huāshēng dòuhuā*). The historic district is very close to the Anping Port (安平港, *ānpíng gǎng*). As such, the seafood here is very fresh.

Although it is true that you can find just about any food dish almost anywhere in Taiwan, southern Taiwan does have its own unique cuisine. Many of these dishes have been exported to other parts of Taiwan. For example, the popular night market dish, called coffin bread, can be found in many night markets around the island. However, locals will tell you that the best coffin bread can only be found in Tainan. My (Matt) friends and colleagues from Tainan all rave that southern Taiwan has the best food, especially the night market food.

To the south of Tainan is the biggest city in this region, Kaohsiung (高雄, *gāoxióng*), which is the third-largest city on the island. It only takes 2 hours to go from Taipei City to Kaohsiung via high-speed trains.

Taiwan's Diverse Geography   147

Anping Old Fort (安平古堡, ānpíng gǔbǎo). *Image courtesy of Henrietta Yang*

Kaohsiung has an important shipping industry because it has the largest sea port on the island for transporting freight containers. The Kaohsiung port accommodates three-quarters of all shipping containers that move in and out of the island. In addition to the shipping industry, Kaohsiung also has a vibrant fishing industry. Therefore, seafood is a major offering in this city.

In addition to the shipping and fishing industries, Kaohsiung is also a critical military site. Tsoying Harbor (左營港, zuǒyíng gǎng) in the city is

A beach at the southern tip of Taiwan. *Image courtesy of Henrietta Yang*

the only military harbor on the island, which is located within the Tsoying Naval Base. The American navy used to base here.

At the far southern tip of Taiwan is Kenting National Park (墾丁國家公園, *kěndīng guójiā gōngyuǎn*). This is a tourist mecca and Taiwan's version of Hawaii with beachside hotels, resorts, surfing, snorkeling, windsurfing, bicycle rentals, hiking, and so on. The weather is warm and humid, the waves are decent, the beaches beautiful, and the water clear and warm.

OUTLYING ISLANDS

Taiwan has many satellite islands, and the main ones include Penghu (澎湖, *pénghú*), Kinmen Islands (金門, *jīnmén*), Matsu Islands (馬祖, *mǎzǔ*), Liuqiu (琉球, *liúqiú*), and Green Island (綠島, *lǜdǎo*). Except for Green Island, all of them are located between the main landmass of Taiwan and mainland China, which is called the Taiwan Strait. The first three islands are a part of three different archipelagos of islands and islets that form three individual administrative counties, respectively Penghu County (澎湖縣, *pénghú xiàn*), Kinmen County (金門縣, *jīnmén xiàn*), and Lienchiang County (連江縣, *liánjiāng xiàn*). Liuqiu belongs to Pingtung County (屏東縣, *píngdōng xiàn*), while Green Island belongs to Taitung County (台東縣, *táidōng xiàn*).

The Penghu archipelago is the largest one under Taiwan's administrative territory. It is about 31 miles west of Chiayi County (嘉義縣) and is accessible via air and ferry. The largest island and city in Penghu County are both called Magong (馬公, *mǎgōng*). When I (Henrietta) visited the island thirty years ago, the fishing industry was still the island's economic backbone. But when I visited Magong again in 2019, it was obvious that the fishing industry has been replaced by tourism, like many of Taiwan's satellite islands. During the 2019 trip, I took a day trip to nearby islands Qimei Islet (七美嶼, *qīměi yǔ*) and Wang-An Island (望安島, *wàngān dǎo*). The interisland cruise also passed by several islets such as Hujing Islet (虎井嶼, *hǔjǐng yǔ*) and Tongpan Islet (桶盤嶼, *tǒngpán yǔ*), which had interesting rock formations.

Penghu is the most developed and popular offshore option for residents on the main island because of its size and the variety of activities it can offer. When I was there in 2019, I stayed at a Sheraton Hotel. Its interior design, quality, and size was similar to many hotels in Hawaii or other seaport cities in the United States. If you like seafood, you will be in paradise when you visit Penghu. The offerings are fresh, and prices are cheap. People on the island are very friendly and accommodating.

Both the Kinmen and Matsu archipelagos are much closer to Mainland China than to Taiwan. Kinmen Islands (金門, *jīnmén*) lie in Xiamen Bay, roughly 6.5 miles east of Xiamen City of the Fujian Province, which is China's territory, but is about 115 miles from Taiwan's west coast shoreline. Matsu Islands (馬祖), about 138 miles northwest of the main land of Taiwan, is less than 6 miles away from China's territory, even closer to Mainland China than Kinmen. Even though both Kinmen and Matsu archipelagos are important Taiwan military bases because of their close vicinity to Mainland China, tourism has developed into a critical part of the local economy. Unlike Penghu and other islands, which boast a diverse array of activities for tourists, the main attractions of Kinmen and Matsu are cultural and historic sites. Another important economic industry in Kinmen is its famous Kaoliang liquor (高粱酒, *gāoliang jiǔ*), made from fermented sorghum. The alcohol level in Kaoliang liquor is around 58 percent. Drink at your own risk.

Liuqiu is situated in the Taiwan Strait, only about 8 miles southwest of Pingtung County. From the island, you can easily see both Kaohsiung and Pingtung on a sunny day. In the past the island's main industry was fishing, but like the other islands, it has been taken over by tourism. The only way to the island is by ferry from Pingtung County, which only takes about 30 minutes. You can see coral, caves, and rock formations on the island because Liuqiu is a coral island. The most famous rock formation on the island is called Flower Vase Rock. The island also offers a wide variety of activities like swimming, snorkeling, and big green sea turtle viewing.

Green Island is a tiny island in the Pacific Ocean, about 20 miles off the eastern coast of Taitung County. For four decades this island was used to jail many political prisoners under the White Terror from 1947 to 1987. Nowadays, the island is open to the public, and tourism is the main industry, even though there is still a maximum security prison on the island. Travelers can get to the island by air (15–20 minutes) or via ferry (50 minutes), which is the most popular choice for tourists. Many water activities are offered by the locals, such as snorkeling and diving.

Taiwan is small, but it has a lot to offer. Visitors will find sophisticated shopping and cultural centers, natural hiking trails, beautiful gorges, and peaceful sandy beaches. Students will enjoy academic freedom in Taiwan's excellent institutions and Chinese language learning centers. Expatriates will find safe, friendly, accommodating working environments. And foodies will be in a food paradise! Just prepare yourself and have a wonderful time in this Formosa, "beautiful island!"

Table 8.1. Useful Phrases

台北	*táiběi* (Taipei)
北	*běi* (north)
台中	*táizhōng* (Taichung)
中	*zhōng* (middle)
台南	*táinán* (Tainan)
南	*nán* (south)
高雄	*gāoxióng* (Kaohsiung)
花蓮	*shuālián* (Hualien)
台東	*táidōng* (Taitung)
東	*dōng* (east)
新北市	*xīnběi shì* (New Taipei City)
市	*shì* (city)
台北縣	*táiběi xiàn* (Taipei County)
縣	*xiàn* (county)
西門町	*xīméndīng* (Shi-men Ting)
萬華區	*wànhuá qū* (Wanhua District)
區	*qū* (district)
信義區	*xìnyì qū* (Xinyi District)
文創商品	*wénchuàng shàngpǐn* (culturally innovated products)
淡水	*dànshuǐ* (Tamshui)
基隆	*jīlóng* (Keelung)
九份	*jiǔfèn* (Jiufen)
故宮博物院	*gùgōng bówùyuàn* (National Palace Museum)
北投	*běitóu* (Beitou)
陽明山	*yángmíng shān* (Yangming Mountain)
鶯歌陶瓷老街	*yīnggē táocí lǎojiē* (Yingge ceramic old town)
十分	*shífēn* (Shifen)
新竹	*xīnzhú* (Hsinchu)
日月潭	*rìyuètán* (Sun Moon Lake)
阿里山	*ālǐshān* (Alishan)
鳳梨酥	*fènglí sū* (pineapple cakes)
宜蘭	*yílán* (Yilan)
太魯閣國家公園	*tàilǔgé guójiā gōngyuán* (Taroko Gorge National Park)
墾丁國家公園	*kěndīng guójiā gōngyuán* (Kenting National Park)

NOTES

CHAPTER 1

1. Indexmundi, https://www.indexmundi.com/taiwan/literacy.html (accessed June 9, 2023).
2. World Population Review, https://worldpopulationreview.com/countries/taiwan-population (accessed June 9, 2023).
3. National Taiwan Normal University, Mandarin Training Center, http://www.mtc.ntnu.edu.tw/eng/introduction.htm%20 (accessed June 9, 2023).
4. Statista, https://www.statista.com/statistics/1321524/taiwan-number-of-foreign-residents (accessed June 9, 2023).

CHAPTER 2

1. Wikipedia, "Geography of Taiwan," https://en.wikipedia.org/wiki/Geography_of_Taiwan (accessed April 10, 2020).
2. Executive Yuan, R.O.C., "重要統計數據 [Important Statistic Numbers]," https://www.ey.gov.tw/state/51BCA519727F88FF (accessed June 9, 2023).
3. Executive Yuan, R.O.C., "語言文字 [Language and Writing]," https://www.ey.gov.tw/state/99B2E89521FC31E1/691a8eae-8e47-444c-8cde-250931aed459 (accessed June 9, 2023).
4. Wan-Yao Chou, 臺灣歷史圖說 [*An Illustrated General History of Taiwan*] (New Taipei City: Linking Books, 2016), 26–27.
5. Hsiao-Feng Lee, 以地名認識台灣 [*Get to Know Taiwan by Place Names*] (New Taiwan City: Vista Publishing, 2017), 17–18.
6. Indigenous Peoples Cultural Development Centers, "台灣原住民族的起源 [The Origin of Taiwan's Aboriginal Peoples]," https://www.tacp.gov.tw/Aboriginal/AbContent?ID=c404a05c-ad58-4003-9014-137c958837c7 (accessed June 19, 2018).

7. Shung Ye Museum of Formosan Aborigines, https://www.museum.org.tw/ (accessed June 19, 2020).

8. Con-Ziin Yiong, "加強推動客語復振 [Strengthen the Revitalization of Hakka]," *110年全國客家人口暨語言基礎資料調查發表* [2021 National Hakka Population and Language Basic Data Survey Published], *Hakka Affairs Council*, https://www.hakka.gov.tw/Content/Content?NodeID=34&PageID=45419 (accessed April 1, 2023).

9. Language Usage in Taiwan, "Southern Min," https://you.stonybrook.edu/aas220taiwan/chinese-dialects/southern-min/ (accessed November 21, 2021).

10. June Huang, telephone interview with Henrietta Yang, June 17, 2020.

11. Brookings, "Taiwan's 228 Incident: The Political Implications of February 28, 1947," https://www.brookings.edu/events/taiwans-228-incident-the-political-implications-of-february-28-1947/ (accessed June 10, 2023).

12. Cliff Chu, telephone interview with Henrietta Yang, May 11, 2020.

13. Margery Wang, telephone interview with Henrietta Yang, May 18, 2020.

14. Taiwan Public Opinion Foundation, "台灣人的民族認同 [Taiwanese National Identity] (April 26, 2022)," https://www.tpof.org/台灣政治/國家認同/台灣人的民族認同（2022年4月26日）(accessed June 12, 2023).

15. National Immigration Agency, "外籍配偶人數與大陸(含港澳)配偶人數 [The Number of Foreign Spouses and the Number of Mainland (including Hong Kong and Macao) Spouses] (April 2023)," *Ministry of the Interior, R.O.C.*, https://www.immigration.gov.tw/5382/5385/7344/7350/8887/?alias=settled own (accessed June 9, 2023).

16. Laws and Regulations Retrieving System, "國民中小學開設本土語文課程應注意事項 [Matters Needing Attention in Setting Up Native Language Courses in Primary and Secondary Schools] (June 16, 2022)," *Ministry of Education, R.O.C.*, https://edu.law.moe.gov.tw/LawContentHistoryList.aspx?id=FL039252 (accessed October 11, 2022).

CHAPTER 4

1. Steven Crook and Katy Hui-wen Hung, *A Culinary History of Taipei* (Lanham, MD: Rowman & Littlefield, 2018), 104–7.

2. Crook and Hui-wen Hung, *A Culinary History of Taipei*, 50–53.

3. Crook and Hui-wen Hung, *A Culinary History of Taipei*, 153–54.

4. Matthew B. Christensen, *Decoding China: A Handbook for Traveling, Studying, and Working in Today's China* (New Clarendon, VT: Tuttle Publishing), 79–84.

5. Christensen, *Decoding China*, 84–88.

CHAPTER 5

1. Department of Household Registration Affairs, "戶籍人口統計速報 [Quick Report on Household Registration Population Statistics] (May 2023)," *Ministry of the Interior, R.O.C.*, https://www.ris.gov.tw/app/portal/346 (accessed June 11, 2023).
2. "Accommodations and Insurance," Chinese Language Division, Language Center of National Taiwan University, http://cld.liberal.ntu.edu.tw/en/accommodations-and-insurance.html (accessed November 14, 2022).
3. Airbnb, https://www.airbnb.com (accessed November 14, 2022).
4. 7-Eleven Latest News, "統一超商2021年度上半年財報 [Uni-President Supermarket's Financial Report for the First Half of 2021] (August 3, 2021)," https://7-11.com.tw/company/csr/news_detail.aspx?id=797 (accessed October 25, 2021).
5. "Travelers' Health, Taiwan," Centers for Disease Control and Prevention, https://wwwnc.cdc.gov/travel/destinations/traveler/none/taiwan.

CHAPTER 6

1. Research Report, "2009年台灣兒童課後照顧概況調查報告 [2009 Survey Report on After-School Care for Children in Taiwan]," Child Welfare League Foundation, R.O.C., https://www.children.org.tw/publication_research/research_report/2111 (accessed December 1, 2022).
2. Department of Lifelong Education, "111年度全國短期補習班及兒童課後照顧服務中心業務管理暨公共安全研討會 [2022 Annual National Short-Term Tutoring Schools and Children's After-School Care Service Center Business Management and Public Safety Seminar] (October 25–26, 2022)," Ministry of Education, R.O.C., https://depart.moe.edu.tw/ed2400/News_Content.aspx?n=15388506A60ACB81&sms=87137EA6056ADFD1&s=E16A1301EC0E85C6 (accessed June 11, 2023).
3. Publication, "2023-2024 Study in Taiwan: Learning Plus Adventure," Study in Taiwan, https://www.studyintaiwan.org/discover/download (accessed June 12, 2023).
4. Hui-Jing Chou, "教改改出什麼? [What Did the Educational Reform Reform?]" in 逆風台灣：民主開放崎嶇路 我們一起走過 [*Headwind Taiwan: Let's Walk the Rugged Road to Democracy and Openness*], ed. Hui-Jing Chou, Ping Yin, Shu-Qi Chuang, Yi-Ting Lin, and Kai-Yuan Teng (Taipei City: CommonWealth Mag. Publishing, 2018), 76–77.
5. Wei-Fan Kuo, "大學那麼多，要怪選舉 [There Are So Many Universities, the Election Is to Blame]" in 逆風台灣：民主開放崎嶇路 我們一起走過 [*Headwind Taiwan: Let's Walk the Rugged Road to Democracy and Openness*], 74–76.

6. Article, "111年大學錄取率98.94%，缺額逾3成均創新高 [The University Acceptance Rate in 2022 is 98.94%, and the Absentee Rate Exceeds 30%. Both Hit a New High]," Flipped Education, https://flipedu.parenting.com.tw/article/007546 (June 12, 2023).

7. "111學年度大專校院一覽表 [2022 List of Colleges and Universities]," Ministry of Education, R.O.C., https://ulist.moe.gov.tw/Browse/UniversityList (June 12, 2023).

8. Publication, "2023–2024 Study in Taiwan: Learning Plus Adventure" (accessed June 12, 2023).

9. Publication, "2023–2024 Study in Taiwan: Learning Plus Adventure" (accessed June 12, 2023).

10. The MOE *Huayu* Enrichment Scholarship (HES) by the Ministry of Education (MOE), https://tafs.mofa.gov.tw/SchDetailed.aspx?loc=en&ItemId=17 (accessed June 12, 2023).

11. Publication, "2023–2024 Study in Taiwan: Learning Plus Adventure" (accessed June 12, 2023).

12. Publication, "2022 Learning Chinese in Taiwan," Study in Taiwan, https://www.studyintaiwan.org/discover/download (accessed June 12, 2023).

CHAPTER 7

1. Cliff Chu, UMC HR Senior Director, telephone interview with Henrietta Yang, August 25, 2022.

2. Taiwan's LinkedIn, https://tw.linkedin.com (accessed August 24, 2022).

3. 1111 人力銀行 [1111 Human Power Bank], https://www.1111.com.tw/ (accessed August 24, 2022).

4. TUN 大學網 [College Websites], https://university.1111.com.tw/index.asp (accessed August 24, 2022).

5. 104 人力銀行 [104 Human Power Bank], https://www.104.com.tw/jobs/main/ (accessed August 24, 2022).

CHAPTER 8

1. Michelin Starred Restaurants in Taipei, https://en.wikipedia.org/wiki/List_of_Michelin_starred_restaurants_in_Taipei (accessed June 9, 2023).

2. Frontline Formosa, "Taiwan's Dominance in the Chip Market Industry Makes It More Important," *Economist* 2023, https://www.economist.com/special-report/2023/03/06/taiwans-dominance-of-the-chip-industry-makes-it-more-important%20 (accessed June 9, 2023).

3. Council of Indigenous Peoples, "The Tribes in Taiwan," https://www.cip.gov.tw/en/tribe/grid-list/index.html?cumid=5DD9C4959C302B9FD0636733C6861689 (accessed June 9, 2023).

INDEX

Note: Page references for figures and tables are *italicized*.

aboriginal tribes, 18, 19–20, 143
academic freedom, 117
Airbnb, 88
airports, 36–37
Alcon, 125
Alien Residence Certificates (ARCs), 91, 94
Alishan High Mountain Tea, 77
Alishan National Scenic Area, 140
Amis tribe, 143
Anping Old Fort, 146, *147*
Anping Old Street, 147
apartments, 11, 86–87, 88
apps: High Speed Rail (HSR), 38; maps, 36; toll payment, 41; transportation, 104
Atayal tribe, 143
ATM machines, 10, 94
Austronesian languages, 18, 19–20

Bafang Yunji Dumpling, 71
banking, 94
Baoan Temple, 6
beaches, 6–7, *147*, 148
Beigan, 52
Beitou hot springs, 139

bicycle travel, 48–50, *48*, 108, *109*, 139
birth rate, 3
black teas, 76
boba/bubble tea, 77–78, 77
body language, 131
box lunches, 72–73, *73*
breakfast foods, 68, *68–69*
Buddhism, 5, 116
Bunun tribe, 143
business culture, 130–33
bus travel, 37, 41–42, 47–48

Capital Bus, 42
Carrefour, 125
car travel, 37, 41, 42–44
cash, use of, 10, 11
cell phones, 94–95
Central Mountain Range, 135, 140
CET-Taiwan, 119
Chen Shui-bian, 14
Cheng Ho, 12
Chiang Ching-kuo, 13
Chiang Kai-shek, 13, 14, 21, 23
Chiayi, 140–41
Chihpen, 145

China. *See* People's Republic of China (PRC)
Chinese language education, 9, 25, 30, 111, 117–19, 122–24
Chinese New Year, 103
Chishang, 145
Christianity, 5
Chu, Mr., 26
City Café, 97
cleanliness, 7, 12
climate, 1, 120
clothing: climate-appropriate, 120; fashion and dress, 7, 10; office dress codes, 132–33
code-switching, 132
coffee shops, 94
communication styles, 131–32
Communism, 8
Confucianism: in education, 110; temples, 5; values, 2–3, 22
convenience stores, 69–70, *70*, 93, *93*, 95–100, *96*, *97*, *99*
corporations, global, 125
Costco, 125, *125*
cost of living, 11, 118
COVID-19 pandemic, 9, 10
credit cards, 10
crime, 7
cross-strait relations, 15
culture: business, 130–33; diversity, 114–15; foreign influences, 3–4; immersion in, 120–21, 123–24, 133; northern vs. southern cities, 7; traditional Chinese, 116; values, 2–3, 10, 12, 22
culture shock, 32–33
currency exchange, 10
cycling, 48–50, *48*, 108, *109*, 139

debit cards, 10
Deloitte, 125
Democratic Progressive Party (DPP), 13, 14, 15, 26

demographics: aboriginal tribes, 143; Austronesian tribes, 19–20; foreign population, 9; population, 6, 18, 85; residential identities, 17–19, 22–23; Taiwanese identity, 25–29
diversity, 114–15
dormitories, 87–88
driving, 37, 41, 42–44
Dutch invasion period, 12, 19

Eastern Taiwan, 141–45, *142*, *144*
EasyCard, 45, 47, 48
education: after-school learning centers, 107–8; extracurricular activities, 107; industry-academic collaboration, 126–27; traditional Asian paradigms, 110–11; university system, *111*, 112–14; useful phrases, *124*; value of, 105–8. *See also* study abroad programs
educators, 106, 129
elders, respect for, 3
Electronic Toll Collection (ETC), 41
English language use, 4, 115
etiquette: business, 130–33; dining, 82–84; outdoor shoes/indoor slippers, 87
express trains, 39

Facebook, 88–89, 104
"face" issue, 132
FamilyMart, 70, 93, 100
family size, 3
Far Eastern Electronic Toll Collection Co., Ltd. (FETC), 41
fashion and dress, 7, 10, 120, 132–33
fast-food chains, 71–72, *71*
Feng Chia University, 140
ferries, 37, 52–53
filial piety, 3, 22
financial assistance for education, 115–16
fitting in, 30–32. *See also* useful phrases

Flower Vase Rock, 149
food scene: Anping Old Street, 147;
  box lunches, 72–73, 73; breakfast
  foods, 68, 68–69; Chinese fusion,
  57–58, 7; convenience stores,
  69–70, 70; dining etiquette, 82–84;
  fast-food chains, 71–72, 71; foreign
  influences, 60, 60, 114, 115; fruits,
  65–66, 65–67; hot pot, 73–75,
  75; Japanese influences, 3, 4, 58,
  59–60, 72; regional influences, 56;
  restaurants, 79–84, 80–82, 84; social
  life and, 55–56, 58; street food,
  55, 60–64; sweets, 58, 59; Taipei,
  138; tea culture, 76–78, 77; tips for
  eating well, 78; useful phrases, 64;
  vegetarian/vegan cuisine, 75–76;
  Western influences, 60, 71
foreign influences, 3–4, 10, 115
foreign population, 9
Formosa Freeway, 41
Foundation for International
  Cooperation in Higher Education
  of Taiwan, 112, 115, 116
Foxconn Technology Group, 125, 139
freedom: academic, 117; of expression,
  10, 12, 114; of movement, 35
fruits, 65–66, 65–67
Fujian Province, 8, 12, 21, 149
"Für Elise" (Beethoven), 95

Gaomei Wetland Preservation Area,
  140
geography: Eastern Taiwan, 141–45,
  142, 144; Northern Taiwan,
  136–39, 137; outlying islands,
  52–53, 148–49; overview, 6–7,
  135–36; Southern Taiwan, 145–48,
  147; useful phrases, 150; Western
  Taiwan, 139–41, 140, 141
Giant Bicycles, 48, 49, 139
government, 2, 12–14, 26, 85
green education, 26

Green Island, 52, 148, 149
green teas, 76
greeting etiquette, 131
group identity, 22

Hakka Affairs Council, 21
Hakka language, 8, 18, 21–22
Han Chinese, 19, 21
handshakes, 131
Han dynasty, 110
health-care system, 11, 100, 102
High Speed Rail (HSR), 37–38
highways, 41–44
Hi-Life, 93, 93
historical highlights, 12–14
holidays, 102–3
hospitality, 9–10, 12, 122
hotels, 11, 89–91, 90
hot pot, 73–75, 75
hot springs, 139, 145
housing: apartments, 86–87;
  on-campus vs. off-campus, 87–89,
  107–8; costs, 11; hotels, 89–91, 90;
  overview, 85–87, 86
Hsinchu, 139
Hsinchu Science Park, 126, 127
Hualien, 141–45, 142
Hualien Airport, 36
Huang, June, 23–25, 26
Huashen 1914 Creative Park, 138
Huayu Enrichment Scholarship (HES),
  115
Human Power Bank websites, 128–29

identification, personal, 11, 91–92
identity, 17–19, 22–23, 25–29, 34
IKEA, 125
immigrants, 29–30
independence movement, 13, 14, 15,
  25
industrial centers, 6
industry-academic collaboration,
  126–27

insiders, vs. outsiders, 27–29
International Chinese Language Program (ICLP), 9, 118–19
International Higher Education Scholarship Program, 115
international relations, 15
internet access, 12
internships: finding and landing, 126–29; industry-academic collaboration, 126–27; making the most of, 133–34; useful phrases, *134*; via personal connections, 129; websites for finding, 127–29

Jade Mountain, 6
Japanese influences: architecture, 3; business culture, 130; coffee shops, 94; colonial, 13, 19–20, 21, 22, 23–25; cultural, 114; food, 3, *4*, 58, 59–60, 72
Jiaoxi hot springs, 139
Jiufen, 138–39
jobs. *See* work

Kaohsiung, 140, 146–47
Kaohsiung Airport, 36
Kaohsiung Incident, 13
Kaoliang liquor, 149
Kavalan tribe, 143
Keelung, 138
Keelung Miaokou Night Market, 62
Kenting National Park, 6–7, 148
Kinmen Islands, 148, 149
Koxinga, 12, 22
Kuo-Kuang Motor Transportation Company, 42
Kuomingtang Party (KMT), 13, 14, 15, 23–25

languages: Austronesian, 18, 19–20; Chinese Mandarin, 1, 4, 8, 25–27, 30; dialects, 8; English, 4, 115;

Hakka, 8, 18, 21–22; Mother Tongue Policy, 29; National Language Policy, 21, 25, 29–30; Southern Min, 18, 22–23; Taiwanese, 7, 8, 22; useful phrases, *34*; variety spoken, 18–19, 114; written, 8
lanterns, *103*, 139
Lee Teng-hui, 14
Line, 104
LinkedIn, 128
literacy rates, 4, 8
Liú Míng-Chuán, 13
Liuqiu, 148, 149
Liwu River, 143
long-term residency, 91–92

Ma Ying-jeou, 14
Magong, 148
"Maiden's Prayer" (Bądarzewska-Baranowska), 95
mainland China. *See* People's Republic of China (PRC)
Mainlander identity, 25–27
Mandarin, 1, 4, 8, 9, 25, 30
Mandarin Training Center (MTC), 9, 118–19
maps, downloadable, 36
marriage, 29
Mass Rapid Transit (MRT), 35, 36, 44–47, *45–46*
Matsu Islands, 52, 148, 149
media access, 12
medical care, 11, 100–102
medical schools, 112
menus, 79–84, *80–82*, *84*
Ming dynasty, 12, 21
Ministry of Education (MOE), 118; *Huayu* Enrichment Scholarship (HES), 115; Short-Term Research Award (STRA), 116; Taiwan Scholarship, 115

Ministry of Foreign Affairs (MOFA):
  Fellowship, 116; Taiwan
  Scholarship, 115
Ministry of the Interior, National
  Immigration Agency, 29
Miyazaki, Hayao, 139
Mos Burger, 71, *71*
Mother Tongue Policy, 30
mountains, 6, 135, 140
municipalities, 85, *86*. See also specific cities

names, use of personal, 130–31
Nangan, 52
National Central University, 127
National Cheng Kung University, 112, 113, 126
National Chiao Tung University, 112, 126
National Chung Cheng University, 119, 141
National Chung Hsing University, 60, 140
National Health Insurance (NHI), 100, 102
National Language Policy, 21, 25, 29–30
National Palace Museum, 139
national parks, 6–7, 143, 148
National Taiwan Normal University, Mandarin Training Center (MTC), 9, 118–19
National Taiwan University, *109*, 112, 113; Chinese Language Center, 88, 119; International Chinese Language Program (ICLP), 9, 118–19
National Tsing Hua University, 126
National Yang Ming-Chiao Tung University, 112
National Yang Ming University, 112; International Health Program (IHP), 119

neighborhoods, 85, *86*, 92
New Residents, 29–30
night markets, *17*, 55–56, *56*, 60–64, *61*, *63*, 142
Ningxia Night Market, *56*
Northern Taiwan, 136–39, *137*

oolong tea, 76–77
Orchid Island, 52
Oriental Beauty tea, 77
oyster omelets, 57, *57*, 59

parks, 6
passports, 2, 11
payment methods, 10, 11
pearl milk tea, 77–78, *77*
Penghu Islands, 52, 148
People's Republic of China (PRC):
  Chinese identity, 25–29; cross-strait relations, 15; cultural values, 2–3; differences, 2, 7, 10–11; food influences, 56; foreign relocation from, 9; historically, 12–14; language differences, 8; similarities, 1
phones, 94–95
pineapple, 66, *67*, 141, *141*
plum blossom, 41
politics, 2, 12–14, 26
population, 6, 18, 85; foreign, 6
post offices, 92
public service jobs, 107–8
public toilets, 95
public transportation, 6, 8, 11, 35–36, 135
Puyuma tribe, 143

Qimei Islet, 148
Qing dynasty, 12, 21
Qingshui Service Area, 43–44, *43*

rail passes, 40
recycling, 95

religious practices, 3, 5–6, *5*, 12, 116, *117*
rental costs, 11
Republic of China (ROC), 13, 23, 25–27
Research Grant for Foreign Scholars in Chinese Studies, 116
residency, 7
respect, showing, 130–31. *See also* etiquette
rest areas, 43–44, *43*
restaurants, 79–84, *80–82, 84*
ridesharing, 52
Rift Valley, 145
Rukai tribe, 143

safety, 7
scholarships, 115–16
scooters, 50–51, *50*
seasons, 120
service areas, 43–44, *43*
7-Eleven, 70, *70*, 93, 95–100, *96, 97, 99*
shaved ice, 65, *66*
Shifen, 139
Shilin Night Market, 61, *61, 63*
shopping, 138
Shung Ye Museum of Formosan Aborigines, 20
SIM cards, 94–95
size of island, 6, 18, 35
slippers, indoor, 86–87
Smart Fish, 64
social life, food scene and, 55–56, 58
social media, 88–89, 104, 114
Songshen Cultural and Creative Park, 138
Southern Min language, 18, 22–23
Southern Taiwan, 145–48, *147*
Spirited Away (film), 139
Stanford University, 9, 118
Starbucks, 125
STEM graduates, 126–27

street food, 55, 60–64, *61–63*
study abroad programs: benefits of, 114–17; on-campus vs. off-campus housing, 87–89, 107–8; Chinese language programs, 4, 9, 111, 117–19, 122–24; financial assistance, 115–16; making the most of, 120–24; useful phrases, *124*
Sun Moon Lake, 140, *140*
Sun Yat-sen Freeway, 41

Taichung, 139–41
Taichung Airport, 36
Tainan, 58, 145–46
Taipei, 136–39, *137*
Taipei 101 (building), 137, *137*
Taipei City, *2*, 136
Taipei Medical University, 112
Taipei Metro, 44–47, *45–46*
Taipei Songshan Airport (TSA), 36
Taitung, 141–42
Taiwanese language, 7, 8, 22
Taiwan High Speed Rail (HSR), 37–38
Taiwan Province, 23–25
Taiwan Public Opinion Forum, 27
Taiwan Railway, 37, 38–40
Taiwan Railway Administration (TRA), 72
Taiwan Relations Act, 13, 15
Taiwan Semiconductor Manufacturing Company (TMSC), 125, *126*, 139
Taiwan Strait, 148
Tamshui, 138
Taoism, 5, 116
Taoyuan International Airport (TPE), 36
Taroko Gorge National Park, 143–45, *144*
taxi services, 51–52
tea culture, 76–78, *77*
temples, 5–6, *5, 18*, 116, *117*, 143
tempura, 58

tips: for Chinese language studies, 122–24; for eating well, 78; for fitting in, 30–32; making the most of work/internships, 133–34; for staying healthy, 102
TKK Fried Chicken, 71
tolls, 41
Tongpen Islet, 148
Traditional Chinese Medicine (TCM), 101–2
train travel, 37–40
translations. *See* useful phrases
transportation, 6, 8, 11, 35–36, 135; buses, 37, 41–42, 47–48; cycling, 48–50, *48*, 108, *109*; driving, 37, 41, 42–44; ferries, 37, 52–53; flying, 36–37; metro system, 44–47, *45–46*; ridesharing, 52; scooter riding, 50–51, *50*; taxi services, 51–52; trains, 37–40; useful phrases, *53*
trash collection, 95
traveling outside of Taiwan, 121
Treaty of Shimonoseki, 13, 22
Tsai Ing-wen, 14
Tsoying Harbor, 147
tuition costs, 115–16
Tunghai University, 140
228 Incident, 25

Uber, 52
Ubike/Youbike, 48–50, *48*
Ubus, 42
"ugly American syndrome," 31
United Microelectronics Corporation (UMC), 126–27, *127*
university system, 4, 112–14
useful phrases: breakfast foods, *68–69*; daily life, *104*; education, *124*; geography, *150*; language and identity, *34*; restaurant menus, *80*, *81*, *82*, *84*; street food, *64*; transportation, *53*; work/internships, *134*

values: cultural, 2–3, 10, 12, 22; educational, 105–8
vegetarian/vegan cuisine, 75–76
Vietnamese, 29
visa requirements, 10, 12, 91

Wang, Ms., 27
Wang-An Island, 148
weather, 120
websites: access to, 12, 114; apartment hunting, 88–89; Facebook groups, 89; fellowships and scholarships, 115; High Speed Rail (HSR) tickets, 38; hotels, 91; job-searching, 127–29
Wenhua Road Night Market, 64
Western influences, 2, 7; business culture, 130; coffee shops, 94; food, 60, 71
Western Taiwan, 139–41, *140*, *141*
White Terror period, 13, 14, 25, 149
work: business culture, 130–33; finding and landing jobs, 126–29; housing options, 87–89; industry-academic collaboration, 126–27; job-searching websites, 127–29; making the most of, 133–34; public service jobs, 107–8; useful phrases, *134*; via personal connections, 129. *See also* internships

Xi Jinping, 14, 15
Xiamen Bay, 149

Yangming Mountain, 139
Yilan, 141–42, 145
Yingge ceramics, 139
Youbike/Ubike, 48–50, *48*

Zhèng Chénggōng, 12, 22

ABOUT THE AUTHORS

Matthew B. Christensen is professor of Chinese at Brigham Young University (BYU) where he has been teaching for the past twenty-eight years. He is also director of the BYU Chinese Flagship Center and has been working with that program since 2002. He has directed and managed flagship and study abroad programs at Nanjing University since the late 1990s.

Henrietta Yang, PhD, is associate professor of Chinese and linguistics and former co-director of the Chinese Language Flagship Program at the University of Mississippi from 2013 to 2021. Yang has directed and managed study abroad programs at Shanghai University in China and National Chung Cheng University and Tamkang University in Taiwan for more than ten years.

Printed in the USA
CPSIA information can be obtained
at www.ICGtesting.com
LVHW040726241223
766638LV00001B/1